"*Time to Lead* is a solid, veritable "how to" on leadership. The approach outlined is straightforward and contains easy to follow, no nonsense instructions on engaging employees in workplace processes. It directly aligns with our organization's transformation to be mission based, metric driven, process oriented and market focused with employee engagement as a key business driver."

—Mark A. Cerkvenik, Director, Organizational Development, Maywood, Illinois

"Mike Cohen has done it again. *Time to Lead* delivers an actionable book on how to have a meaningful conversation with employees about shared expectations with achievable results. Mike knows today's leadership challenges, and he gives thoughtful commentary that truly resonates. This book is a just-in-time reference. It is also an effective management development resource, allowing you to compare your own leadership skills with the best employee engagement practices."

—Sharon Schultz, Vice President of Patient Care Services, Oceanside, CA

"*Time to Lead* is filled with illustrations that are reflective of actual behaviors in the work place. The tools provided are terrific for purposes of building a cohesive team and solving work unit problems. The book serves as a reminder of why I wanted to be a manager in the first place: to make a positive difference on behalf of my employees and customers."

**—Christine Craig, Nursing Director,
Rancho Mirage, CA**

"Time to Lead is a tremendous "how-to" resource for managers at all levels within the organization. The Intergroup Role-Negotiation Exercise really works. We held a Role-Negotiation session as described in the book which resulted in positive and sustained change. And Mike Cohen's Assertive Fair-Fighting Techniques turned co-workers in conflict into collaborative teammates."

**—Nancy N. Donner, PharmD, Director
Pharmacy Services, Aurora, IL**

"Terrific team building exercises! I've used the Problems versus Realities process with different work units in the hospital. It definitely works. Employees successfully addressed challenges that were within their control to overcome. Equally important, they stopped complaining about those inherent work frustrations that no one can do anything about."

**—Brett Wakefield, Vice President, Human
Resources, Melrose Park, IL**

"Time to Lead provides exceedingly practical advice on how to improve employee relationships and the quality of customer service. I can't wait to share these exercises with my team. This book is a valuable resource for both new and seasoned managers, providing useful tools for building trust and team cohesiveness."

**—Marie A. Cleary-Fishman, Director of
Performance Improvement, Naperville, IL**

"My unit utilized the team development exercises contained in *Time to Lead*. During the team building sessions many eyes were opened. All of the participants (nurses, health unit coordinators, OB technicians and physicians) benefited from the unique activities. The accountability concepts and emphasis on follow through were especially helpful. This new book adds another dimension to an already great tool kit."

—Margaret Malnory, Administrative Director, Women and Children's Services, Racine, WI

"*Time to Lead* provides managers with goal focused and task-oriented team development exercises to actively engage employees. The book focuses on how to improve communication within and between work units to achieve seamless customer service. It is an excellent guide for creating a positive work environment in which the employee is viewed as an internal customer."

—Lorraine Harris, Director, Human Resources, Waukegan, IL

TIME
TO
LEAD

TIME
TO
LEAD

The Ultimate Guide
to Employee Engagement

MICHAEL   HENRY   COHEN

CREATIVE

HEALTH CARE

MANAGEMENT

ISBN 13: 978-1-886624-84-9

Cohen, Michael Henry.
Time to lead: the ultimate guide to employee engagement / by Michael Henry Cohen.
      p. cm.
Includes bibliographical references.
ISBN 978-1-886624-84-9 (pbk. : alk. paper)
1. Leadership. 2. Management. I. Title.

HD57.7.C638 2011
658.4'092—dc22

            2011003652

Printed and bound in the United States of America

First Printing: March 2011

15 14 13 12 11   5 4 3 2 1

For permission and ordering information, write to:

CREATIVE

HEALTH CARE

MANAGEMENT

Creative Health Care Management, Inc.
5610 Rowland Road, Suite 100
Minneapolis, MN 55343-8905

chcm@chcm.com
or call: 800.728.7766 or 952.854.9015

www.chcm.com

*This book is dedicated to the Chicago Cubs,
who throughout my lifetime have taught me the virtue of patience
and the capacity to accept (expect) everyday frustrations,
yet remain hopeful for a better tomorrow.*

CONTENTS

II

A Focus on Values

III

A Focus on Team Development

Contents

MY STORY

When I was Director of Employee Relations and Development at Weiss Memorial Hospital in Chicago, I conducted leadership development workshops and led team building activities within and between departments. Responsible for the hospital's recruitment and retention program, I coached employees who were in conflict with their manager or co-workers and coordinated the organization's formal grievance process. I was the hospital's equal employment opportunity officer, ensuring that every hiring decision, promotion, performance appraisal and corrective action was administered in an ethical and legal manner. Finally, I served as the liaison between the executive staff and the employees, facilitating effective organizational communications.

I loved the nature, function and scope of my job. It was a perfect match for my educational background, work history and skill set. While I was at Weiss, I wrote a book based on my experiences entitled *Employee Handbook for On-The-Job Survival: Practical Advice For Dealing With Everyday Work Problems*. This book put me on a national speaker's tour, and as a result, I received requests to conduct workshops within other organizations.

At about the same time the University of Chicago Hospitals, located on the south side of Chicago, acquired Weiss

Memorial Hospital to get a foothold on the north side of the city. Shortly thereafter, the vice president of human resources resigned. The new CEO, who knew of my consulting work at the University of Chicago, promoted me to the vacated vice president position.

At first I was flushed with pride and enthusiasm about my new role, but it didn't take long to realize that this job was not for me. I was so consumed with administrative responsibilities, I no longer had time for activities that I excelled in and enjoyed. Moreover, the hospital was bleeding red ink and I had to coordinate three successive reductions in staff. One of the cuts included my previous job, the director of employee relations and development.

The managers who survived the organizational restructuring now found themselves with more employees to supervise and a wider span of control. Everyone felt stretched to the max. Both managers and staff had a palpable sense that the quality of customer service and employee morale was slipping.

To complete my various tasks, I came to work early and left for home late every day. By the time I got home, I felt wasted. I needed to decompress before I could fully engage in quality time with my wife, Jo Ellen, and our three children. Frequently, I took work home with me just to keep up and I was always accessible to co-workers during off hours. On vacations I would check in to see how things were going.

With the promotion, I received a 20% increase in pay, and I had relative job security. (I wasn't going to lay myself off.) Yet I was not a happy person and was in real danger of burning out. At first, I was in denial. Jo Ellen finally had to level with me. She reminded me how much I once enjoyed my job and how I used to talk with her about what was happening at work. Now I kept silent. I used to get up for work every morning with enthusiasm. Now I had trouble getting out of bed. I used to come home with a smile on my face. Now I came home looking despondent.

She observed that the only time I had a gleam in my eyes was when I was preparing for a workshop outside the hospital. And when I came home from an external consulting job, I actually appeared energized. She suggested that I consider leaving Weiss to become an independent consultant, to engage in an activity that I actually enjoyed.

My first response was defensive. I replied, "There's no job security as a consultant. We have three children to support. College payments are just around the corner. And don't forget the mortgage. After all, I am making more money than ever, and I enjoy my relative job security."

She responded, "Well I'm not standing in your way. I want to see you happy. Sure, it's a risk. There are no guarantees that it will work out, but sometimes not taking a risk is the greater risk. I don't want to see you wake up one day when it's too late, wondering if you could have been successful doing what you really love. If necessary, we can always lower our standard of living. But you need to be engaged in work that is meaningful and satisfying, not only for your sake but for your family's."

On an intellectual level, I knew that she was right. I would never become a great vice president of human resources because I had no passion for it. But emotionally, I wasn't able to cut the cord yet. It took another few months to act. Finally, I approached the new CEO and negotiated a graceful separation from the hospital.

That was many moons ago. Today I am president of my own leadership and organizational development consulting company, and I have never looked back. I am making more money than I would have if I stayed at Weiss, but more importantly there is a real sense of purpose and fulfillment in my work.

I have come to the conclusion that there are no guarantees for job security. No one is entitled to a lifetime of employment within the same organization. And sometimes the price you pay for the illusion of job security is cynicism and unhappiness.

I have learned that job success and satisfaction come from:

- Enjoying the fundamental nature, function and scope of your job.

- Having a clear challenge that fully engages and stretches your abilities.

- Possessing the talents and skills to overcome work challenges.

- Taking pride in your accomplishments by creating a high quality product or service that is of value to others.

- Receiving recognition from people you value. (But ultimately, your motivation must be intrinsic. If it's a job worth doing, it's worth doing well.)

- Having the opportunity to grow both personally and professionally.

- Enjoying a positive relationship with your co-workers, manager and customers.

To be successful and satisfied on the job, you need to choose a career that is a good match for your strengths and desires, and then find an organization that will pay you for what comes naturally. The money will follow. And although you may not become rich, you will be enriched, because your work will be in alignment with your God-given talents.

Follow your bliss!

—Michael Henry Cohen,
Author, Consultant and Speaker

SUMMARY OF TERMS

Time to Lead:

Time is a very precious commodity. How you spend it is a reflection on your values. Effective leaders choose their priorities carefully based on their vision for the work unit. Then they exert personal influence to facilitate employees' success at realizing this vision. In the process they:

- Encourage/guide

- Educate/coach

- Challenge/exhort

- Advocate/support

- Galvanize/energize

- Engage/listen

Employee Engagement:

Effective leaders spend a significant amount of time on their work unit making themselves accessible and approachable to employees. They observe first-hand the ebb and flow of activities, and they are available to immediately respond to situations that demand their attention. Their communication with employees is open, honest and respectful.

Build Trust:

Effective leaders maintain credibility with employees by keeping their promises and honoring their commitments. Leaders demonstrate that they have the best interest of their employees in mind. They strive to be fair and consistent in the application of personnel policies and performance management decisions. Through their words and deeds, leaders earn employees' confidence.

Develop Teamwork:

Leaders strive to enhance relationships within and between shifts, job classifications and work units. They focus on team goals that transcend personality conflicts, turf battles and individual self-interests. Effective leaders select and retain only those employees who are good team players. They understand that it takes just one toxic personality to negatively impact the work unit's culture.

Exceed Customer Expectations:

Leaders engage in a sustained and relentless pursuit of service excellence. Employees know that this is a non-negotiable expectation and a condition of employment.

The key to effective leadership today is influence, not authority.

Kenneth Blanchard

INTRODUCTION

A leader's primary responsibility is to create a positive work environment that facilitates employees' job success, recognizes and holds people accountable for outstanding results, and helps employees look good in the eyes of the customer. Effective leaders believe that if you don't serve the customer directly, your job is to serve those who do.

To be successful in this endeavor, leaders spend quality time on the work unit actively engaged with employees, monitoring and evaluating their activities, providing timely performance feedback and offering a helping hand when the need exists. They play the roles of positive change agent, coach, team builder and facilitator of continuous quality improvement.

Effective leaders regularly utilize employees as internal consultants in decision making processes that directly impact their work. They actively listen to employees to understand their needs, expectations and hopes. They informally negotiate with employees on how to best serve the interests of the customer.

The Challenge of Becoming an Engaged Leader

Current economic conditions have been the catalyst for organizational restructuring and reductions in staff. This has resulted in fewer leaders with a greater span of control and more employees to supervise. Many of the activities in which leaders are expected to participate include organizational maintenance responsibilities that take them away from the work unit. These include:

- Administrative tasks

- Management meetings

- Committees

- Reports

- Projects

- Crises

The leader's absence from the work unit for extended periods of time has created an environment in which employees lack direction and support. In response to this dilemma, some leaders have attempted to empower their employees by providing them more authority and autonomy in their jobs.

Unfortunately, some employees lack the skills, maturity, motivation or work ethic to function independently. And, while these high-maintenance employees act perfectly fine when the leader is present, their mischief begins as soon as the leader is called away from the work unit.

The *Time to Lead* Philosophy

The quality of performance, teamwork and customer service almost always improves when a respected and competent leader is present on the work unit to directly supervise activities. This is not to suggest that leaders should spend their time hovering over employees watching every move they make, nor is it recommended that they dictate how everything gets done.

Employees who have earned the leader's trust should be provided the appropriate amount of freedom to make decisions and take independent action. But freedom without responsibility can be a very dangerous thing. Therefore, high-maintenance employees need to be monitored more closely. This requires leaders who are present and actively engaged with employees on the work unit.

Engaged leaders define the objectives and (with guidance) let employees find their own route to accomplishing them. The leader doesn't care so much about *how* employees meet their goals, providing they do so in an ethical, professional and legal manner. Employees are held accountable for results, not necessarily how they achieve those ends.

As an engaged leader you are not actually managing employees, they are managing themselves and you are managing their performance. You provide the vision, the resources to succeed and the standards by which employees will be evaluated. They either have the will and the skill to meet performance expectations or they don't. You have no control over employees. You can't make them do anything. What you do have is control over the consequences of their decisions.

Book Overview

Engaged leaders:

- Choose priorities that are in alignment with their values.

- Establish leadership credibility as a precondition for effective employee engagement.

- Select a leadership style that meets the needs and expectations of employees.

- Facilitate team development to achieve seamless customer service.

- Include employees in decision making processes on issues that directly impact their work.

- Ensure that meetings with employees are constructive and productive.

- Recognize employees in a manner that reinforces desired behavior.

- Evaluate candidates for employment based on their technical competence, teamwork orientation, customer service skills and emotional intelligence.

About the Team Building Activities

Some team development exercises provide valuable insights into the personal dynamics of a work unit. They are very effective at exploring employee values, communication and work style differences. They artfully probe into personal relationships and their impact on how a group functions. These exercises are tested and proven as a means to improve teamwork.

However, the team development exercises contained in this book avoid probing into personal feelings. Employees are not asked to disclose their innermost thoughts about one another as if the unvarnished truth will set them free and absolute honesty is a virtue. There are no games, role playing, holding hands or group hugs. Employees are not asked to sing *Kumbaya* together.

On the contrary, the exercises within this book are goal-focused and task-oriented. They are based on a simple premise: regardless of how an employee might feel toward a co-worker, the work unit mission transcends personality conflicts, turf battles, and differences in communication and cultural style. Each person has a role to play in setting up co-workers for success and helping them look good in the eyes of the customer.

Achieving good employee relations is not a primary work unit goal. It is a means to an end. That is, good relationships grease the results channels for exceeding customers' expectations. A work unit can't provide seamless service unless all team members effectively communicate and cooperate with one another.

This book is designed to be a practical resource for both new and seasoned managers. It is not overly theoretical or academic. The intent is to provide common sense and down-to-earth information that you can immediately apply within your work unit. It's all about getting back to basics.

Enjoy the read and good luck on your journey to employee engagement!

I

A FOCUS ON CREDIBILITY

Nearly all men can stand adversity, but if you want to test a man's character, give him power.

Abraham Lincoln

1

MANAGEMENT VERSUS ENGAGED LEADERSHIP

As a manager, your primary role is to serve as the guardian of organizational resources and expenditures. This includes the coordination of employee activities to accomplish specific objectives. Your responsibilities are to:

- **Organize:** Decide how and when tasks will be accomplished.

- **Deputize:** Identify roles and assign tasks.

- **Supervise:** Ensure that tasks are completed on schedule in accordance with standards of performance.

To facilitate your success, the organization grants you the authority to tell people what to do, enforce policies and procedures, evaluate performance and mete out consequences for inappropriate conduct.

The organization provides you this authority so that you can turn potential chaos into order and ensure that the system runs smoothly. Organizations are inherently bureaucracies, and managers are bureaucrats. Managers protect the status quo. They make certain that work is completed in a timely and efficient manner.

However, it is important to remember that your position's power is not really yours. The organization has loaned you this power for the time being. And anything the organization gives, it can also take away. Therefore, a manager's power is inherently transient.

The Nature, Function and Scope of Engaged Leadership

As an engaged leader, you do not rely on your authority to achieve positive outcomes. Employees follow you not because they fear you, but because they identify with you and your vision for the work unit. Your credibility is established by simply telling employees who you are and what you're about. Then you become that person. You lead by example, which is the highest form of leadership. You remain true to your values and steadfast in your pursuit of excellence.

You are effective because you are worthy of belief and confidence. Your own conduct denotes a strict adherence to honesty and trustworthiness. You are perceived to be genuine. Employees are comfortable with you because you demonstrate good manners, temperament, voice control and appropriate choice of language.

Your positive influence springs from your ability to pull people together, to clarify objectives and make them understood. Employees know that you are totally committed to them and to the success of the team. In the last analysis, positional power, credentials or degrees don't make you a leader. Your leadership is established only by performance and verifiable results achieved through ethical conduct, decisions and language.

A Paradigm Shift from Management to Enlightened Leadership

Since the 1960s there has been a significant change in how we think about the leader-employee relationship. There has been a shift:

- From command decisions to consensus-building.

- From a task orientation to a focus on results.

- From motivation through fear to positive reinforcement and individual responsibility.

- From leaders having all the answers to utilizing employees as internal consultants in the decision making process.

- From record-keeping and documenting mistakes to coaching for success.

- From an unstated vision and assumed values to the open sharing of purpose.

Of course it is sometimes necessary to use your positional power to meet work unit objectives. Disapproval, constructive criticism, reprimand and forced compliance are among the leader's tools available to achieve results. But if you rely on these as your primary strategies for getting what you want, the result will be work relationships characterized by polarization, breakdowns in communication, distrust and fear.

Leader as Coach

This book contains many team development activities to improve customer and employee satisfaction within your work unit. Team building is analogous to sports teams; therefore, you can benefit from modeling the behaviors of successful coaches.

Baseball coaches, for example, focus on helping players continuously improve their job performance and enhance their skills. They instill fundamentals by helping team members know how to play their particular positions, including what to do and when to do it.

Coaches build teamwork by making sure all players know how their individual roles interweave with others on the team; they evaluate and adjust when necessary. For example, they will reposition players, change the game plan and respond to an individual's changing needs.

Coaches remain encouraging and supportive when a player is going through a rough stretch or the team is on a losing streak. When the team begins to doubt its ability to win, coaches intervene to instill confidence. They become trusted advisers to their players. They provide additional training to help them get out of their slump.

Coaches defend their players when criticized by the media and take complete responsibility for the team's problems. Through the ups and downs of a season (or career), a special bond typically develops between the coach and the players that can last for a lifetime.

Coaches demand that when it's time to play the game, players leave their personal problems behind them, put on their game faces and play to the best of their abilities. They expect players to make sacrifices for the good of the team. If players can effectively perform on the field, they are expected to play hurt providing it doesn't aggravate an existing injury.

Above all, successful coaches agonize over the recruitment and selection of personnel. A team will never realize its full potential unless the coach hires and retains only the most talented players available. During spring training, the coach places people in positions where they can excel, evaluates their talent and makes cuts as required. Both new and long-term players have to compete for their jobs; longevity doesn't count. Through this process, only the most talented people get to wear the uniform.

Maintaining a positive relationship with players is very important, but ultimately a coach's job security depends on quantifiable results largely determined by the team's win-loss ratio. Coaches are expected to get their teams into the playoffs on a consistent basis. Their legacy depends on achieving the ultimate goal of winning the championship.

Like a successful coach, you select and retain the best available employees. By placing them in positions where they can contribute, you provide encouragement, skill development and accountability for results.

Listed below are additional characteristics of leaders who have established personal and positional power. Complete this checklist to evaluate your leadership credibility.

A Checklist to Determine if You Are a Credible Team Leader

Yes   **No**

☐   ☐   I demonstrate enthusiasm and a steadiness of purpose.

☐   ☐   I say positive things about my job, co-workers and work unit.

☐   ☐   I make those around me feel motivated and important.

☐   ☐   I work well with a variety of people including those of different personalities, work styles, cultures and experiences.

☐   ☐   I create a retribution-free communication environment in which employees are encouraged to play the role of devil's advocate without fear of retaliation.

☐   ☐   I make myself approachable and accessible.

☐   ☐   I secure resources and permissions from above to facilitate employees' success.

☐   ☐   I support employees under fire. I have their backs.

☐   ☐   I avoid publicity, fame, honors and celebrity.

☐   ☐   I demonstrate humility.

Yes   No

☐   ☐   I enjoy recognizing and rewarding others for their talents, efforts and positive results.

☐   ☐   I credit employees when things go well and take complete responsibility when things go wrong.

☐   ☐   I enjoy making things more efficient, productive, user-friendly, neat, simple, fast, safe and cost-effective.

☐   ☐   I support my own manager and other organizational leaders by casting a positive light on difficult or unpopular decisions.

☐   ☐   My work unit has developed a reputation for outstanding customer service. We consistently exceed our customers' expectations.

☐   ☐   Team morale is high.

☐   ☐   I attend to three fundamental psychosocial needs of employees:

- The need to be appreciated.
- The need to be heard.
- The need to be understood.

Based on this self-assessment, you may want to consider positive behavior changes to enhance your leadership credibility.

Five Levels of Power

Your influence within the work unit springs from five levels of power:

1. **Position Power:** People follow you because they *have to.* They fear the consequences of non-compliance.

2. **Relationship Power:** People follow you because they *want to.* They are drawn to the force of your personality, character and ability to pull people together in pursuit of a common goal.

3. **The Power of Achievement:** People follow you because you have a history of accomplishments. They have confidence in you and want to be a part of your work unit's success.

4. **The Power of High Expectations:** People follow you because you will not tolerate mediocrity. This is how you attract and retain the best employees.

5. **The Power of Support:** People follow you because you are there for them when they need you. You are accessible and approachable. You have their backs. You are committed to their well-being.

Discussion Questions

Are management and leadership roles mutually exclusive? Can you be effective at one and not the other?

Think about an outstanding leader in your life (a boss, coach, teacher, etc.) and identify the characteristics you admired most in this person. Describe how the person made a positive difference in your life.

Think about a terrible leader with whom you have worked and identify the characteristics that you disliked the most.

Integrity without knowledge is weak and useless,
and knowledge without integrity is
dangerous and dreadful.

Samuel Johnson

THE MASTER OF
LEADERSHIP

Aristotle, the Greek philosopher and teacher, wrote the
foundational book on leadership entitled *Rhetoric* (Greek for
"persuasion"). In this classic text, Aristotle presents three
modes of influence to facilitate a change in an audience's
thinking or behavior:

1. Logos

Speak with authority. Demonstrate mastery over your
subject matter by presenting an argument that is factual,
logical, reasonable and correct. Provide documentation to
support your conclusions.

Aristotle says that if the truth is on your side, and the
truth is irrefutable, use it to your advantage. Logos is the
science that deals with rules or tests of sound thinking. It is
the proof that leads your audience to believe that you are

reasonable and thorough about your recommended course of action.

In other words, to be influential you must be perceived by your employees as someone who has the requisite knowledge and technical expertise to be their leader.

2. Pathos

Know your audience. Align your argument with their perceived needs and expectations. Appeal to the "better angels" of the audience's natures by focusing on their:

- Compassion

- Pride

- Loyalty

- Sense of fair play

- Altruism

- Hopes and dreams

Or, you can demagogue an issue through the audience's fears and prejudices by focusing on their:

- Hatred and propensity to scapegoat

- Insecurity

- Greed

- Frustration and anger

- Sense of victimization

- Jealousy

History is replete with leaders who have been very effective in the short run appealing to the worst instincts in people. Charisma placed in the wrong hands can be a very dangerous thing.

Pathos appeals to either the enlightened or individual self-interests of your audience. When you appeal to their enlightened self-interests, you demonstrate how your plan is advantageous to the work unit or organization. It is consistent with your mission, vision and values. When you appeal to their individual self-interests, you tailor the argument to each person's unique needs (perceived or real).

In other words, to be influential you must be perceived by employees as someone who is understanding of and sensitive to their attitudes, feelings and beliefs.

3. Ethos

Demonstrate that you are a trustworthy source of information. In particular, show that you possess:

- **Intelligence and Wisdom:** You have the requisite mental capacity and common sense to be their leader.

- **Virtue:** You are a person of integrity and honesty.

- **Good Will:** You care about your employees' well-being. You are supportive of them.

- **Generosity:** You are motivated to achieve win-win outcomes as opposed to exhibiting conduct that smacks of self-aggrandizement, ego tripping or grandstanding.

In other words, to be influential you must be perceived by employees as a person who is trustworthy and a decent human being.

The lessons of Aristotle's *Rhetoric* are clear: in the art of persuasion, it's not the message that is crucial—it is the messenger. If you don't first establish credibility with your employees, they will be reluctant to accept any of the changes that you introduce to improve work unit functioning. If employees don't trust you, they will resist all of your compelling emotional appeals. All of your logic, reason and fact-based rhetoric will fall on deaf ears. Your employee engagement initiatives will be thwarted if they perceive you to be deceptive, manipulative, overbearing or simply out of touch with the realities of the work unit.

How to Lose Support and Alienate Your Employees

If there is any discrepancy between what you preach and what you do, employees will scrutinize your behavior more closely than anything you say. They will harbor resentment because of the glaring double standard and hypocrisy you represent.

Like it or not, there exists a higher standard of conduct for leaders than for employees. You are being paid to remain cool, calm and collected, particularly in stressful conditions. You must model the attitudes and conduct expected of employees.

Listed below are leadership behaviors that result in a breakdown in communication, distrust and polarization. Use this checklist for self-assessment purposes.

Yes   No

☐   ☐   I bad-mouth one employee to another.

☐   ☐   I violate confidences.

☐   ☐   I use employees as a sounding board to criticize my boss, another manager or work unit.

☐   ☐   I criticize employees publicly, providing no opportunity for them to save face or keep self-esteem intact.

☐   ☐   I engage in angry outbursts (yelling, swearing, pounding the table).

☐   ☐   I attack employees personally by calling them names ("you're incompetent," "you're lazy," "you're stupid," "you're unprofessional").

☐   ☐   I act aloof or arrogant.

☐   ☐   I view employees as useful tools for getting the job done, but want little to do with them beyond that.

☐   ☐   I exhibit an aggressive, controlling management style.

☐   ☐   I flaunt my position power by constantly reminding employees who's the boss.

Yes **No**

☐ ☐ I treat certain employees coldly, silently or abruptly by snubbing, ignoring and dismissing their concerns.

☐ ☐ I provide glaring eye contact or "the look" (a testing and evaluative glare of impatience, distrust or contempt).

☐ ☐ I blame or discredit employees without first listening to their perspective and investigating their side of the story.

☐ ☐ I sit idly by when employees need an extra hand, refusing to roll up my sleeves and get my hands dirty when the need exists.

☐ ☐ I exhibit erratic mood swings from day to day (patiently listen to employees' concerns one day and then bite their heads off the next for no apparent reason).

☐ ☐ I take credit when things are going well and blame employees when things go wrong.

☐ ☐ I practice preferential treatment (favoritism).

☐ ☐ I preach one thing but do another (take extra-long coffee breaks, come to work late and leave early, etc.).

Based on this assessment, consider choosing one or more items that represent an opportunity for improvement, and develop strategies for positive behavior change.

A Special Word to the New Leader: Potential Pitfalls to Avoid

As a new leader, you may be eager to make a positive impact on the work unit by introducing a myriad of changes to improve operating efficiency. As a result of your desire to immediately set things right, you risk:

- Ignoring work unit strengths.

- Imposing changes that employees are not yet ready to accept.

- Communicating the unintended message that all decisions made by the previous manager are suspect.

- Traumatizing the work unit with change overload.

Patience is a virtue. Unless you are mandated from above to make immediate and sweeping changes, you should first take whatever time is required to understand the history and culture of the work unit.

A Note to the Leader Promoted from Within

If you are a leader promoted from within the work unit, you face a particular set of challenges. Now you have to supervise your former peers, some of whom might be your best friends. You have to assign them work, evaluate their performance and administer corrective action when necessary.

Some employees may:

- Accuse you of changing: "The power has gone to your head."

- Scrutinize and second-guess every decision you make.

- Claim that you are not carrying your fair share of the workload.

- Challenge your authority (refuse to accept an assignment).

- Resent taking direction from someone much younger than themselves.

- Question your qualifications for the job.

You may begin to doubt your own abilities and wonder if accepting the promotion was a mistake. In an attempt to be accepted by employees, you may tolerate mediocre performance and disrespectful conduct. As a result, you abdicate your leadership responsibilities and compromise your values.

Once you accept a promotion from within your work unit, it is important to accept the fact that things will never be the same between you and your former peers. The responsibilities of your leadership position will fundamentally change the nature of the relationship.

New Leader's Needs Assessment Exercise

Whether you are a leader who is new to the organization or are making the transition from co-worker to leader, consider engaging in the following employee needs assessment exercise. It will help you understand employees' expectations and provide valuable information on how to proceed as an effective change agent.

STEP ONE:

Meet with employees on an individual basis. Explain that you want them to serve as internal consultants on how to create a positive work environment that facilitates their job success and satisfaction. Ask them the following questions:

- "What are the strengths of the work unit?"

- "What are the opportunities for improvement?"

- "If you were in my shoes where would you begin to make changes?"

- "How can we best get employee ownership of these changes?"

- "What are your expectations of me as your manager?"

STEP TWO

Meet with your employees as a group to:

- Summarize the results of your interviews.

- Articulate your vision for the work unit.

- Share your ideas for moving forward.

- Describe the leadership style that you intend to embrace.

STEP THREE:

Identify those employees on your work unit who can most help or hinder the accomplishment of your goals. These are your work unit's opinion leaders. Identify the personal and professional qualities they possess that cause co-workers to seek out their advice on various work unit issues.

Think about the *positive opinion leaders* and how you can:

- Place them in a pivotal position to be more influential.

- Utilize them as consultants in your decision making processes.

- Prepare them for future management positions.

Next, think about how you can establish a better relationship with the *negative opinion leaders*. Identify what you can do to:

- Co-opt them so that they are working with and not against you.

- Turn their cynicism into healthy skepticism.

- Better understand what motivates them.

- Recognize and build on their strengths.

- Ask them to help you advance a strategy for improving work unit functioning.

- Give them a role to play in the process.

For Longer-Term Leaders: An Employee Negotiation Exercise

Engaged leaders don't wait for the results of an annual employee satisfaction survey to find out what employees are thinking. They regularly seek feedback about themselves and informally negotiate with employees about how to improve the working relationship. Consider using the following exercise to facilitate this process.

STEP ONE:

Meet with your employees as a group, and present the following two lists:

- "These are the things I have tried to do to create a positive work environment that facilitates your job success and satisfaction…"

- "Based on your previous feedback, I believe you would like me to stop doing (do less of) or start doing (do more of) the following things to make your job easier, more satisfying and effective…"

After presenting the two lists, ask for employee feedback:

- "In what ways am I being too hard or easy on myself?"

- "Is there anything else you would like me to do differently to better meet your needs?"

- "What information would you like that you're not getting?"

- "What decisions have I made in the recent past in which you would have appreciated an opportunity for input before the decision was made?"

- "Are there any changes in the near future about which you want to be consulted?"

- "How can I facilitate improvement in the quality of communication within the work unit?"

- "What training and development needs are not being met?"

It is critical that you don't get defensive upon receiving employee input. Your employees' perceptions, accurate or not, are real and you have to deal with them.

STEP TWO:

- Share with employees a list of what they are currently doing to make your job easier, more satisfying and effective.

- Next, share with employees what you want them to start or stop doing to better meet your needs and expectations.

(Alternative Approach for Step Two):

- Have employees develop their own lists of what they think they are currently doing to meet your needs and expectations.

- Have employees make lists of what they can do differently to make your job easier and more satisfying.

- Share with employees the ways in which they are being too hard or easy on themselves.

STEP THREE:

Based on this structured dialogue, you and the employees generate commitments for positive change that you are willing and able to honor. It is critical that you follow through on these commitments; otherwise you will raise false expectations which can result in distrust and cynicism.

The following is an example of commitments a leader and employees made to one another to make each other's jobs more satisfying and effective:

Leader's Commitments to Employees

- Whenever possible, I will ask for your input on any decisions that impact the work unit.

- I will promote positive employee relations within and between work units by not bad-mouthing one employee, shift or work unit to another.

- I will encourage direct communication among co-workers in conflict and will not get in the middle of every conflict.

- I will not make promises that can't be kept. I will provide you regular status reports on any commitment that I make.

- I will encourage feedback about my conduct, and promise not to retaliate against anyone who provides me constructive criticism.

- I will do whatever is possible to make available equipment, materials and supplies. When requests are made for resources I am not able to provide, I will honestly communicate this in a direct, straightforward manner.

- I will provide you with ongoing feedback on critical performance issues to minimize surprises on your annual appraisals.

Employees' Commitments to Leader

- We will come to you about problems without whining about them. We will try to come up with solutions to the problems that we identify. We will listen to your point of view.

- When you do something that upsets us, we will talk to you, not about you.

- We will not do end runs to HR. We will follow the chain of command.

- We will try to resolve conflicts with one another in a direct and respectful manner. When appropriate, we will ask you to coach us on how to provide feedback in a constructive fashion.

- We will accept your constructive criticism without getting defensive.

- We realize that you need positive feedback as much as we do. Therefore, we will let you know when you do something that makes our job more satisfying and effective.

Lessons from the Tao of Leadership
Adapted from Lao Tzu's *Tao Te Ching*

- Nobody has all the answers. Acknowledging that you don't know is far wiser than acting as if you do. It is a relief to say, "I don't know."

- The wise leader is not motivated by collecting a string of successes. The leader helps others find their own success. There is plenty to go around.

- The wise leader knows that the reward for doing good work arises naturally out of the work, that style is no substitute for substance, that possessing certain facts is not more powerful than wisdom.

- Do you want to be a positive influence in the world? First get your own house in order. Your influence begins with you and ripples outward.

- It is a mistake to believe that a great leader is above others. Paradoxically, greatness comes from knowing how to be receptive and how to be of service.

- A centered leader is not subject to passing whims or sudden excitements. Being grounded means being down to earth, having gravity: "I know where I stand. I know what I stand for."

- It is not easy to understand a person whose foundation is invisible.

- We are all team players. Power comes through cooperation, independence through service, and a greater self through selflessness. The wise leader keeps egocentricity in check.

- The wise leader grows more and lasts longer by placing the well-being of all above the well-being of self.

- Learn to lead in a nourishing manner, without being possessive; to be helpful, without taking the credit.

- Trying too hard produces unexpected results.

- Trying to rush matters gets you nowhere.

- Trying to appear brilliant is not enlightening.

- Center and ground give the leader stability, flexibility and endurance.

Discussion Questions

Why is modeling the attitudes and behavior expected of employees the highest form of leadership?

_____

_____

_____

_____

People don't care how much you know until they know how much you care. What are some of the ways you can show that you care about employees?

_____

_____

_____

_____

Do you believe that establishing your personal credibility is a precondition for successful employee engagement? Please explain.

_____

_____

_____

_____

How do you communicate to employees difficult or unpopular decisions made from above? How do you demonstrate support for employees, yet remain loyal to upper level management?

_____

_____

_____

_____

The first step to getting the things you want out of life is this: Decide what you want.

Ben Stein

CHOOSE AN EFFECTIVE
LEADERSHIP STYLE

There has been a trend over the years to democratize organizational life with an emphasis on project or matrix management. Everybody needs to be a part of every decision before it is implemented. This process can get very time-consuming. It can also lead to role ambiguity that almost always contributes to interpersonal conflict.

The irony is that many employees actually prefer a more traditional, hierarchical management model in which you leave them alone to do their work and don't ask them to play an active role in decision making processes. More frequently than ever, you hear employees say:

"Thanks for the opportunity to become a member of this committee. But honestly, I would prefer to be left alone to focus on those specific responsibilities for which I have been hired. Just make a decision, and tell me what you want me to do."

This sentiment would seem to suggest that you allow employees to do what they were hired to do, want to do and are good at doing. Or at the very least, choose a leadership style that takes into consideration the extent of employees' readiness and desire to be active participants in decision making processes.

Four Leadership Style Choices

Listed below are four leadership style choices beginning with a management-controlled approach and ending with employees being more involved in making decisions that will impact their immediate work environment.

Level One: Leader Makes a Unilateral Decision

In this leadership style, you maintain complete control over the decision making process. You single-handedly:

- Identify a problem and commit to solving it. You determine that the status quo is unacceptable and a change is necessary.

- Secure an understanding of the nature and scope of a problem.

- Explore the advantages and disadvantages of available solutions.

- Choose the best solution.

- Announce the decision (without making any real attempt to gain employee acceptance of the decision).

- Assign responsibilities for implementation.

- Answer employee questions if deemed appropriate.

While you may take into consideration what you think are employees' opinions and feelings on the issue, you don't provide them an opportunity to participate directly in the decision making process. Your decision is final and non-negotiable.

When Unilateral Decision Making is Appropriate/Necessary

Unilateral decision making is most often utilized when the following conditions exist:

- The team has no time to deliberate. There is only a small window of opportunity to act before it's too late. Someone needs to take command of the situation. Therefore, you announce the decision and discuss it later.

- The decision is handed down from above. As the manager, you have no say in the matter.

- You have already made up your mind as to the best course of action. You would be very uncomfortable going in a different direction. There is no point in creating the illusion of a democratic process by trying to manipulate a preconceived outcome.

- The nature of the problem does not lend itself to group decision making. Objective studies suggest that there is only one correct course of action. Regardless of employee sentiment, any other decision will lead to a compromised result.

- You have very little confidence in the employees' ability to solve this problem. They lack the cohesiveness, mutual acceptance and commonality of purpose. Or, they don't have sufficient knowledge and competence with respect to the problem.

- You have identified one person with the specialized knowledge, skill set or interest who can effectively investigate the problem and advance a proposal.

Disadvantages of Unilateral Decision Making

There are significant downsides to using unilateral decision making as your primary leadership style. Many employees naturally resent being left out of decisions that directly impact their work unit. Furthermore, it is more difficult for them to understand, let alone support, management decisions when they are excluded from the decision making process.

Unilateral decision making also creates employee dependence on you for improving work unit functioning. Employees become conditioned to believe that it is their job to identify problems and your role to fix them. It's always easier for employees to gripe about your response to work unit problems when they are not held responsible for suggesting solutions in a constructive and collaborative manner.

Level Two: Leader Sells the Decision

Even when it is necessary to engage in unilateral decision making, it is still important to get employees' understanding and acceptance of the change. Therefore, if time is available, it is incumbent upon you to make a persuasive case for your decision:

- Describe the nature and scope of the problem.

- Explain the negative impact it is having on employees, customers or the organization.

- Articulate how your decision will solve the problem.

- Anticipate and plan for possible ambivalence or resistance to your decision, and shape your presentation in a manner that will satisfy those concerns.

- Announce the decision. Invite questions and engage in "give-and-take" with employees. Provide them a full explanation of your thinking. While you are willing to answer questions and even entertain employees' objections, your decision is final and non-negotiable.

Level Three: Leader Tests Out the Solution with Employees

Nobody has a corner on the truth. We all look at the world through our own lens. Therefore, it is generally a good idea to get employees' opinions before you settle on a final decision.

Whenever time is limited and you can't engage in an extensive participative process, invite employees to play the role of devil's advocate. In this approach, you:

- Identify a problem and commit to solving it. The status quo is unacceptable.

- Secure an understanding of the nature and scope of the problem.

- Explore the advantages and disadvantages of available solutions.

- Select a tentative solution.

- Present your tentative solution and explain its benefits.

- Invite employee feedback on the decision:

  - "What are the potential disadvantages of my proposed solution?"

  - "Will it solve this problem, but create new ones?"

  - "Does anybody have a better solution?"

- Consider the advantages and disadvantages of employee suggestions and then make a final decision.

- Seek employee input on how to best implement the decision.

In this decision making model, it is stipulated that change is necessary and non-negotiable, but you are not wedded to any one solution. You are prepared to refine your ideas or seriously entertain better suggestions to improve the situation. This style of problem solving provides employees the opportunity to exert some limited influence on the decision making process.

Level Four: Leader Encourages Full Participation in the Decision Making Process

This approach represents the greatest opportunity for employees to have input into decisions that impact their work unit. Still, you have choices regarding how much control employees will have in the decision making process. Listed below is a continuum of choices ranging from tight management control to allowing the greatest possible employee input on decisions.

Relative Management Control:

You present a problem without providing any specific ideas for solving it. You ask employees to propose solutions. You consider their input, but you reserve the right to make the decision and develop implementation steps.

More Opportunity for Employee Participation:

You present a problem and ask employees to propose solutions. You consider their input, make the decision and charge employees with the responsibility for developing implementation steps.

Or you can provide even more opportunity for input by presenting a problem to employees and giving them the authority to decide on a solution (providing it meets specific criteria). Employees then recommend implementation steps.

Most Opportunity for Employee Participation:

Employees identify a problem, establish criteria for choosing the best solution, make a decision and develop implementation steps. In this model, you can decide to:

- Facilitate team meetings.

- Delegate the facilitation role to an employee and participate as an equal member of the team.

- Choose not to be directly involved in the deliberations.

Advantages of Employee Involvement

There are numerous benefits to utilizing employees in decision making processes that directly impact their work. Among these are:

- Employees' motivation increases because they feel more in control of their work environment.

- Employees are more likely to embrace the change because they helped create it.

- Because employees are the ones closest to the work, their ideas are more likely to be practical and grounded in reality.

- Employees will effectively implement the steps necessary to solve the problem because they had a say in developing the methods and timetables for completion.

- If the solution does not work out, employees are less likely to blame the manager because they have a greater sense of ownership for success.

Requirements for Effective Participative Decision Making

Recognize that there are certain preconditions for a full employee participative leadership style (Level Four) to work. Use the following checklist to evaluate your employees' readiness to fully engage in decision making processes:

Yes　**No**

☐　☐　Employees view participation in problem solving activities as an inherent part of their job.

☐　☐　Employees understand and take ownership of team mission, vision and goals.

☐　☐　Employees are genuinely interested in the problem and are motivated to solve it.

☐　☐　Employees are provided clear-cut objectives and direction to facilitate solving the problem.

☐　☐　Employees have the necessary knowledge and experience to address the problem.

☐　☐　Employees have been trained in effective problem solving, decision making and conflict management skills.

☐　☐　Employees understand the difference between problems (within the group's control to solve) and realities (outside the group's ability to positively impact).

☐　☐　Employees desire to make things better. They want what is best for the team and its leader.

If these conditions don't exist, you may want to consider a more controlling leadership approach. But make it a goal to create the conditions necessary for employees to succeed in a participative management style. Employees' engagement in decision making processes may take more time than a management-controlled approach, and it can be messy. But in the long run, it can save time. And again, the more input employees have in decisions on issues that impact their work, the more likely that they will take ownership of the decision and effectively implement it.

You can facilitate employees' readiness to engage in a participative decision making process by:

- Engaging in one-on-one employee discussions to access opinions and build trust.

- Creating a retribution-free communication environment.

- Conducting team development workshops.

- Holding all employees accountable for constructive behaviors on the work unit.

When Employees Feel Powerless:

- Their job belongs to the organization. There exists no sense of personal ownership.

- They do what is required, nothing more and sometimes less.

- The job has very little meaning to them other than as a source of income.

- They don't contribute much at meetings because they believe anything they say won't matter. (They complain before and after meetings.)

- Their quality of performance slips when a manager is not present to monitor activities.

- They don't know how to independently manage co-worker conflict and set limits on passive-aggressive or aggressive personalities on the work unit.

- They focus more on their rights than their responsibilities.

When Employees Feel Empowered:

They own their jobs. They do good work not simply because they seek praise from their manager. They perform well out of a sense of professionalism. They sincerely believe that any job worth doing is worth doing well.

- They take pride in being a member of their team.

- They do the right thing when no one is looking.

- They take complete responsibility for their conduct.

- They are more likely to participate in the problem solving process, embrace decisions and effectively implement them.

- Because they have more control over their work, they learn to perform independently and address problems as they occur.

Discussion Questions

Recall recent changes within your organization or work unit that called for a unilateral decision making process. What was the outcome?

_____

_____

_____

_____

_____

Recall recent changes within your organization or work unit that called for a more participative approach to decision making. What was the outcome?

_____

_____

_____

_____

_____

Can you think of a time when the wrong decision making style was chosen? What approach would have been more successful given the nature of the problem?

_____

_____

_____

_____

_____

_____

How can you encourage employees to become more actively involved in helping solve work unit problems? How do you hold them accountable for lack of constructive participation?

_____

_____

_____

_____

_____

_____

It is the province of knowledge to speak and it is the privilege of wisdom to listen.

Oliver Wendell Holmes

AUTHENTIC LISTENING: THE HIGHEST FORM OF RESPECT

Engaged leaders utilize their employees as internal consultants. They spend a significant amount of time listening to employees, accessing their opinions and attitudes on issues that affect the work unit. By listening, leaders develop a better understanding of employees' knowledge, skill sets, personalities, ambitions, goals, problems, pressures and interests. Listening creates a relationship based on mutual respect and cooperation.

Listening to employees' divergent points of view leads to high quality decisions: through the free marketplace of competing ideas, the truth marches forward. Instead of relying on the power of one individual's personality or position, a clearinghouse of opinions creates a healthy check-and-balance system. This process results in merit-based decisions informed by the collective wisdom and experience of the group.

The art of listening includes asking relevant and probing questions:

- "What advantages can you see in doing the job this way?"

- "What might be the best way of rolling out this program?"

- "How can we best package this decision for employees who are most likely to resist it?"

- "Why do you think our decision didn't work out as planned? Was it a fault in the design or implementation?"

- "Before we go ahead with this, let's think of reasons why not to make the change."

Effective listening often requires that you probe as deeply as necessary to ensure you understand the meaning behind the message:

- "Could you please provide me an example?"

- "Is there anything else?"

- "Tell me more about that."

- "You say that you would like me to be more supportive. What would that look like? Please be as specific as possible."

Listening to the words is not enough. For example, you can also observe employee behaviors that could indicate ambivalence or resistance to your ideas:

- Closed body language (folding arms, lack of eye contact, eye rolling, agitated facial expression)

- Sneers, sighs, sarcasm

- Refusal to speak

- Constant interruptions

- Raising of voice/rate of speech

Of course, you must set limits with employees who exhibit disrespectful behavior. But eventually you have to address the root causes of the resistance. Your job is to:

- Listen past words to meaning.

- Listen for the emotions behind the words.

- Listen for answers to the questions you ask.

When you don't listen to employees, it's all too easy to jump to conclusions, make hasty decisions and commit yourself to actions that are ill-advised. When you don't listen, employees believe that you don't care about them as thinking and feeling individuals—that their role is simply to follow directions and not ask any questions. These perceptions ultimately lead to employee complacency, resentment and feelings of victimization.

Listening Can Reduce Tension and Resolve Conflicts

Providing employees a structured forum to express their feelings can clear the air of tension and hostility. You should not tolerate passive-aggressive or aggressive employee conduct. Nor should you entertain gripe and dump sessions that place you on the defensive. However, within the proper context, allowing employees a chance to constructively talk through their feelings can help put things in perspective and clarify expectations. This in turn can lead to more reasonable behaviors.

When employees are angry, demanding or unreasonable, their most fundamental need is to be understood, not necessarily agreed with. Therefore, if you want them to be more understanding of your point of view, the best strategy is to first listen to employees with complete attentiveness. Ask questions to clarify meaning. At various times, insert remarks such as:

- "I understand."

- "Yes."

- "Go on."

- "Please tell me more about that."

Use nonverbal gestures to confirm that you're listening, such as affirmative nods and direct eye contact. Allow employees to fully develop their thoughts without interruption. After they are finished speaking, check to ensure that you heard them correctly:

- "Let me paraphrase what I heard you say."

- "Did I correctly describe the problem from your perspective?"

If their answer indicates that you captured part, but not all, of their concerns, ask for clarification. Even if you strongly disagree with what they're saying, communicate that you can appreciate their perspective. This is the meaning of empathy:

- Get inside their heads, and look at the situation from their worldview.

- Sense the employees' anger, suspicion, confusion or feelings of being treated unfairly.

- Appreciate the fact that their beliefs (right or wrong) are perfectly reasonable and legitimate to them.

Clarify employee expectations by asking what they would like you to do to remedy the situation. They may only want you to understand their situation but not take any action. Or they may want you to do something to help solve the problem. Assess your ability and willingness to meet their expectations. If appropriate, explain your constraints and limitations. Be prepared to explore various options for meeting their needs.

Authentic listening takes time. It is also very difficult to do when you are put on the defensive. For example, employees may blame you for something that you didn't do, or they may insist you solve a problem that is outside your control. But that's when effective listening is most needed. It's easy to be calm when employees have realistic expectations and are acting in a professional manner. The real test of your character and integrity is how you operate under duress. When others are trying to drag you in the mud, can you maintain the high ground?

The following poem reminds us that sometimes we have to reach out to the very people who seem not to want or need our understanding. It was written in the late 1960s by Charles C. Finn, a former high school teacher in Chicago. He has graciously allowed it to be reprinted in its entirety.

Please Hear What I'm Not Saying

Don't be fooled by me.
Don't be fooled by the face I wear
for I wear a mask, a thousand masks,
masks that I'm afraid to take off,
and none of them is me.

Pretending is an art that's second nature with me,
but don't be fooled,
for God's sake don't be fooled.
I give you the impression that I'm secure,
that all is sunny and unruffled with me, within as well
    as without,
that confidence is my name and coolness my game,
that the water's calm and I'm in command
and that I need no one,
but don't believe me.
My surface may seem smooth but my surface is my mask,
ever-varying and ever-concealing.
Beneath lies no complacence.
Beneath lies confusion, and fear, and aloneness.
But I hide this. I don't want anybody to know it.
I panic at the thought of my weakness exposed.

That's why I frantically create a mask to hide behind,
a nonchalant sophisticated facade,
to help me pretend,
to shield me from the glance that knows.

But such a glance is precisely my salvation, my only hope,
and I know it.
That is, if it's followed by acceptance,
if it's followed by love.
It's the only thing that can liberate me from myself,
from my own self-built prison walls,
from the barriers I so painstakingly erect.
It's the only thing that will assure me
of what I can't assure myself,
that I'm really worth something.
But I don't tell you this. I don't dare to, I'm afraid to.
I'm afraid your glance will not be followed by acceptance,
will not be followed by love.
I'm afraid you'll think less of me,
That you'll laugh, and your laugh would kill me.
I'm afraid that deep-down I'm nothing
and that you will see this and reject me.

So I play my game, my desperate pretending game,
with a facade of assurance without
and a trembling child within.
So begins the glittering but empty parade of masks,
and my life becomes a front.
    I idly chatter to you in the suave tones of surface talk.
I tell you everything that's really nothing,
and nothing of what's everything,
of what's crying within me.
So when I'm going through my routine

do not be fooled by what I'm saying.
Please listen carefully and try to hear what I'm not saying,
what I'd like to be able to say,
what for survival I need to say,
but what I can't say.

I don't like hiding.
I don't like playing superficial phony games.
I want to stop playing them.
I want to be genuine and spontaneous and me
but you've got to help me.
You've got to hold out your hand
even when that's the last thing I seem to want.
Only you can wipe away from my eyes
the blank stare of the breathing dead.
Only you can call me into aliveness.
Each time you're kind, and gentle, and encouraging,
each time you try to understand because you really care,
my heart begins to grow wings—
very small wings,
very feeble wings,
but wings!

With your power to touch me into feeling
you can breathe life into me.
I want you to know that.
I want you to know how important you are to me,
how you can be a creator—an honest-to-God creator—
of the person that is me
if you choose to.
You alone can break down the wall behind which I tremble,
you alone can remove my mask,
you alone can release me from my shadow-world of panic,

from my lonely prison,
if you choose to.
Please choose to.

Do not pass me by.
It will not be easy for you.
A long conviction of worthlessness builds strong walls.
The nearer you approach to me
the blinder I may strike back.
It's irrational, but despite what the books say about man
often I am irrational.
I fight against the very thing I cry out for.
But I am told that love is stronger than strong walls
and in this lies my hope.
Please try to beat down those walls
with firm hands but with gentle hands
for a child is very sensitive.

Who am I, you may wonder?
I am someone you know very well.
For I am every man you meet
and I am every woman you meet.

by Charles C. Finn,
September 1966

Used with permission. This poem and other writings can be
found at: www.poetrybycharlescfinn.com

Discussion Questions

Do you believe that authentic listening is the highest form of respect? Please explain.

_____

_____

_____

Do you spend enough time listening to your employees on a person-to-person basis or in group settings? If not, how are you going to lock this important activity into your schedule?

_____

_____

_____

_____

Are there employees on your work unit who seem to resist any effort to build positive relationships? What can you do to remove their "masks" of indifference or hostility? In addition, what can you do to hold them accountable for constructive conduct despite their personal problems?

_____

_____

_____

_____

II

A FOCUS ON VALUES

There are many ways to avoid mistakes, but the best way to sidestep the disasters is to be available.

T. Boone Pickens

CHOOSE YOUR ACTIVITIES WISELY

Are you spending an inordinate amount of time on bureaucratic or organizational maintenance tasks? Is it increasingly difficult for you to focus on those activities that are of immediate value to customers and employees? Do your employees assert that you are out of touch with what's taking place on the work unit? Are they saying:

- "Where is our manager when a helping hand is needed?"

- "We need someone with the authority right now to deal with a dysfunctional employee who is raising havoc on group morale. Can anyone find our manager?"

- "Our manager spends all of her time in the office behind closed doors or away from the work unit attending meetings. We don't know when it's appropriate to interrupt her."

- "We have a customer who is demanding to speak with the manager. Where is he?"

To what extent would employee and customer satisfaction improve if you spent more quality time on the work unit? How much more fulfilling would your own job become if you were to engage in the following activities on a regular basis?

- Practice MBWA (Management by Wandering Around).

- Make structured customer and employee rounds.

- Address customer and employee complaints on a timely basis.

- Monitor and evaluate outcomes with your own eyes and ears.

- Provide sincere and appropriate compliments to employees immediately following an event that is worthy of praise.

- Offer "Just in Time Coaching": place a resource in employees' hands just before they can use it. Observe employees in action. Provide immediate performance feedback.

- Respectfully confront employees on the spot for their dysfunctional conduct.

- Roll up your sleeves and offer a helping hand when needed.

Are You At Risk for Burnout?

Burnout is not the result of working long and hard hours for sustained periods of time. It comes from working very hard on activities that are of little value to you, such that goal achievement provides you little satisfaction. When you're in a state of burnout, you feel like you're on a treadmill, running very fast, only to remain in the same place. You come to work early, leave late and take work home with you, but you rarely achieve a sense of completion.

Complete the questionnaire below to determine if you are a candidate for burnout.

Yes   **No**

☐ ☐   I often consider my work to be overwhelming.

☐ ☐   I rarely feel a sense of accomplishment.

☐ ☐   It is difficult for me to find uninterrupted time to accomplish important tasks.

☐ ☐   I often feel harried or am reacting to events outside my control.

☐ ☐   I frequently work long hours just to keep up.

☐ ☐   I frequently experience stress due to unfinished work.

☐ ☐   I often work in the evenings and on weekends.

☐ ☐   My work is preventing me from enjoying quality time with significant others. Personal relationships are being compromised by my work.

Yes	No	
☐	☐	I find it difficult to take vacations and feel guilty when I do.
☐	☐	I resent the amount of work associated with my job.
☐	☐	I frequently feel guilty because the quality of my work is slipping.
☐	☐	I often put off doing difficult or unpleasant yet necessary tasks.
☐	☐	I don't have the time or energy to exercise on a regular basis.
☐	☐	I find it difficult to get a good night's sleep. I frequently awake exhausted.
☐	☐	I frequently harbor doubts that I am well suited for this job.

If you answered Yes to at least five of the statements above, you may want to examine whether your activities are in alignment with your values, and think about how you can achieve a better work-life balance.

Are You Suffering from Cognitive Dissonance?

Whenever you are engaged in conduct that is inconsistent with your core values, you are likely to be thrust into a state of cognitive dissonance. Your behavior, which is at odds with your belief system, leads to a crisis of conscience and internal conflict.

The potential for cognitive dissonance is high when the activities that consume your day do not reflect your values or the priorities for your work unit. The only way to alleviate the distress is to bring your activities into alignment with your values, or change your values to make them more consistent with your activities. This is sometimes referred to as rationalization: to reduce anxiety, you find a way to justify your time management decisions and compromise what you stand for.

When deciding how to spend your time, it is an error in judgment to focus on speed or productivity before you determine direction. For example, it is very frustrating to engage in an activity for a sustained period of time only to find out later that you were working on the wrong thing.

Steven R. Covey, in his book, *First Things First*, suggests that when determining your priorities, it is critical to create a vision of what you want to have accomplished and imagine what that vision will look like when realized. To be a leader who accomplishes great things, this must be a lofty vision—one that challenges employees to perform at high levels.

When your vision has been communicated, understood and embraced, employees will not get distracted by personality conflicts or turf battles. Their focus will be on accomplishing goals that require cooperation and a healthy service orientation. When you stay focused on this exalted vision, you won't react to whatever is urgent, the impulse of the moment or other people's definition of a crises.

Identify Your Key Results Areas

If you have 101 priorities, all of them important, you have no priorities because you have no focus. You don't have enough time to excel in everything. Therefore, you want to identify a few Key Results Areas (KRAs) to focus on that are in alignment with your values. For example, many leaders value the following four KRAs and engage in specific activities associated with them:

Customer Relations

Activities:

- Regularly communicates to employees the importance of providing outstanding customer service.

- Creates unit-based standards of conduct for service quality.

- Develops a user-friendly monitoring and evaluation system to measure customer satisfaction.

- Shares customer service feedback with employees and engages in continuous quality improvement activities.

- Trains and develops employees on customer relations skills.

- Provides resources and removes system barriers that serve as impediments to outstanding customer service.

- Spends quality time with customers, soliciting feedback and troubleshooting as indicated.

Teamwork

Activities:

- Creates formats for one-on-one employee relationship building.

- Conducts unit-based staff meetings in which employees are included in decision making processes on issues that directly impact their work.

- Shares information with employees so they understand the context in which they perform their work.

- Ensures effective communication and cooperation between shifts, job classifications and work units.

- Provides status reports on various projects, follows through on commitments made and secures closure on issues.

- Develops work unit protocols for managing conflict.

- Teaches employees how to deal with aggressive and passive-aggressive (victim-oriented) co-workers.

- Recognizes employees for achievement.

- Coaches, counsels and develops performance improvement plans as indicated.

Technical Competence

Activities:

- Creates a learning culture in which employees are expected to be technically competent and clinically sound.

- Conducts thorough new employee orientations within the work unit.

- Identifies employee strengths and development needs.

- Provides one-on-one coaching and continuing education programs, then monitors and evaluates outcomes.

- Establishes new learning objectives at the end of every performance appraisal to ensure that employees are state-of-the-art and cutting-edge in their respective fields.

- Participates in one's own professional development.

Administrative/Maintenance Responsibilities

Activities:

- Develops and adheres to a budget.

- Orders a sufficient quantity of materials and supplies.

- Makes out schedules/attends to staffing issues.

- Engages in project work.

- Completes reports.

- Responds to changing priorities and mandates set from above.

- Attends management meetings.

- Participates on committees/task forces.

- Responds to crises and system breakdowns.

Values Exercise

Are your activities in alignment with your values? Rank these four Key Results Areas (Customer Relations, Teamwork, Technical Competence and Administrative/ Maintenance Responsibilities) in order of **how much they mean to you**. Place the most important Key Result Area first:

1. _____

2. _____

3. _____

4. _____

Now, rank the Key Results Areas in order of **how much time you actually spend on each**. Place the KRA that you spend the most time on first:

1. _____

2. _____

3. _____

4. _____

If the rankings are not the same, you might want to meet with your manager to negotiate a better use of your time. The next chapter will provide you a practical strategy to prepare for such a meeting and discuss how you can bring your work activities into alignment with your values.

Discussion Questions

Are you in danger of cognitive dissonance or burnout because the way you are spending your time is not in alignment with your values?

_____

_____

_____

_____

What specific activities would you like to spend more/less
time on?

_____

_____

_____

Measure your life: it just does not
have room for so much.

Seneca

6

NEGOTIATE PRIORITIES WITH YOUR BOSS

Effective leaders are successful politicians. They have learned the skills of "managing up," obtaining permissions and resources from above to achieve positive outcomes. In particular, it is critical that you and your manager reach an understanding on the best use of your time. Consider using the following exercise to attain agreement on your work priorities.

Time Management Negotiation Exercise

STEP ONE:

Prepare for the Meeting

Review your calendar to identify how you spent the majority of your time during the past 90 days. Ask yourself the following questions:

- What goals did I accomplish or make significant headway on?

- Was accomplishing these goals the best use of my time?

- What goals did I not have time to work on?

- What kept me from working on them?

- Did I take the time for renewal and reflection (big-picture thinking)?

- Did I take the time for my own professional development?

- Was I engaged enough with my employees and customers? Was I there for them?

STEP TWO:

Meet with Your Manager

Discuss those activities that you would like to spend more or less time on. Be prepared to explain how a new set of priorities would make a positive difference for your work unit and organization.

STEP THREE:

Develop S.M.A.R.T. Goals

Specific: Identify those specific activities you will spend more/less time on.

Measurable: State how results will be measured. Outcomes should be quantifiable, observable or verifiable in some way.

Achievable: Demonstrate that success probability is high and the degree of effort is reasonable.

Relevant: Explain how the goal is consistent with the mission, vision and values of the organization.

Timely: Identify when the goal will be met. This may include the identification of specific action steps and time frames associated with them.

An Exercise for Upper Level Managers

As an upper level manager, you must be very mindful of those activities for which you recognize and hold middle and lower level managers/supervisors accountable. What you reward or penalize your managers for is a clear signal of what is important to you and is an indication of how you want them to spend their time. Therefore, it is critical that you bring resources, rewards and accountability systems into alignment with your organizational values.

STEP ONE:

Facilitate better time management among your managers by engaging in the following activities:

- Teach effective delegation skills.

- Provide administrative support for managers whenever appropriate.

- Set realistic deadlines.

- Reduce projects that keep managers off their work units.

- Have managers write reports that are actually read and acted upon.

- Avoid "programs of the month" which are very time-consuming for managers, yet yield little return on investment.

- Ensure that the annual performance appraisal for managers places a significant weight on customer satisfaction, employee relations and technical competence.

- Reinforce a healthy life-work balance.

STEP TWO:

Help your managers develop a sense of purpose and direction by engaging in the following lines of inquiry:

- Why do you want to be in a leadership position?

- Specifically, what do you want to accomplish?

- What do you want your legacy to be when you leave this position? What do you want people to say about you?

- Starting now, what habits do you need to cultivate to realize your full potential as a leader? What will you start (do more) or stop (do less) to achieve your goals?

- What obstacles (internal or external) stand in the way of success? What steps will you take to overcome these obstacles?

- Do you have feelings of frustration or failure in any particular area?

- What do you need from me to facilitate your success?

- How long do you envision being in this position?

- Are there areas within the organization where you believe you can make a significant contribution if given an opportunity?

- If you were in my position, what Key Results Areas would you focus on?

STEP THREE:

Some managers have a difficult time letting go of those activities that they are good at and enjoy doing. Or, they simply have trouble assigning tasks to employees. Have your managers examine the following common myths about delegation:

- "Delegation takes too much time. To achieve positive results, I have to train and develop my employees, monitor and evaluate outcomes, recognize achievement, correct mistakes, coach or discipline. It's simply easier to do it myself. At least I know it will be done right the first time."

- "Employees won't like me if I give them more work. They will think that I am dumping on them."

- "Employees may think that I am not carrying my fair share of the workload."

- "Some employees may refuse to accept the assignment. What will I do?"

- "Employees currently lack the skills to perform the delegated task. I will only be setting them up for failure."

- "I am the one who will be held liable if they make a critical mistake. I can't take that risk."

- "Some employees might perform the task better than I do. I will lose credibility. Next, they may want my job."

Engage your managers in a reality check. Have them analyze each of the above concerns by asking the following questions:

- What is the possibility that these negative outcomes will actually occur?

- What can you do proactively to prevent this negative outcome from occurring?

- How can you best respond if it does happen?

- What will be the negative effects in the long run if you *don't* delegate?

Letting Go

Effective delegation requires that you prepare employees to take over specific tasks, provide them the resources to succeed and hold them accountable for positive results. It requires letting go and trusting the employee to do the right thing.

- To let go does not mean to stop caring. It means you can't do it all yourself.

- To let go is not to forfeit your authority or power. It is to realize that control over another is an illusion. People make their own choices and must live with the consequences of their decisions.

- To let go is not to enable counterproductive behavior. It is to set appropriate limits and abide by them.

- To let go is not to render yourself powerless. It is to understand that the outcome is not completely in your hands.

- To let go is not to be in the middle dictating answers. It is (within parameters) to allow others to decide.

- To let go is not to own everyone's problems. It is to be supportive and to facilitate a positive outcome.

- To let go is not to be protective. It is to permit another to face reality.

- To let go is not to nag or scold. It is to teach and lead by example.

- To let go is not to blame another. It is to encourage and expect individual responsibility.

- To let go is not to adjust everything to your desires. It is to negotiate with others how we can best meet each other's needs.

- To let go is not to regret or feel guilty about the past. It is to learn from your experience, live for the present and prepare for the future.

- To let go is to worry less and plan more.

- To let go is to fear less and trust more.

Caring For Employees versus Taking Care of Employees

Caring for employees is commendable. But taking care of them breeds dependency and resentment.

When you *take care* of employees:

- You do things for employees that they're perfectly capable of doing themselves.

- Your actions suggest to employees that they are unable to solve their own problems.

- Your actions indicate that you are responsible for employees' job satisfaction and motivation.

When you *care for* employees:

- You challenge employees to realize their full potential.

- You tell employees what they need to hear, not necessarily what they want to hear.

- Your primary goal is not to make employees happy. This is not a country club. It's a place of work. Your responsibility is to create a positive work environment that *facilitates* employee job success and satisfaction. But ultimately, employees are responsible for their own motivation, work ethic and positive outcomes.

A Summary of Effective Time Management

- Carefully plan and schedule the use of your time on a daily or weekly basis to ensure that your activities are in alignment with your values. Develop a sense of direction and purpose.

- Negotiate with your manager how to make the best use of your time

- Make time for thinking, planning and creating.

- Delegate appropriate tasks.

- Don't facilitate employee dependency. Let go, and hold employees accountable for positive results.

Discussion Questions

Do you agree with the statement that what managers are recognized or penalized for will strongly influence how they spend their time? Please explain.

_____

_____

_____

_____

Do you have trouble delegating or "letting go?" Please explain.

_____

_____

_____

What specific tasks could you delegate without compromising on results?

_____

_____

_____

_____

III

A FOCUS ON TEAM DEVELOPMENT

If you don't know where you're going,
you might wind up someplace else.

Yogi Berra

ACHIEVE CLARITY OF PURPOSE

To be successful, your work unit must possess a common purpose that transcends individual self-interests, personality conflicts, varying work styles and cultural differences. Performance quality suffers when employees' primary focus is on their own job satisfaction as opposed to the needs of the customer.

Listed below are indicators that employees might have forgotten why they are on the payroll. Use it as a check list. Are these characteristics found on your work unit?

Yes   No

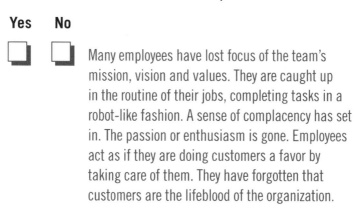

Many employees have lost focus of the team's mission, vision and values. They are caught up in the routine of their jobs, completing tasks in a robot-like fashion. A sense of complacency has set in. The passion or enthusiasm is gone. Employees act as if they are doing customers a favor by taking care of them. They have forgotten that customers are the lifeblood of the organization.

Yes   No

☐   ☐   Many employees are consumed by turf battles, personality conflicts, and differences in communication and work styles. As a result, customer service is being compromised.

☐   ☐   Many employees act as if they are entitled to their jobs. They believe that it's their right to be employed within your organization.

☐   ☐   Many employees view themselves as victims and captive to their situation. They are constantly griping and dumping. They are obsessed with everything that they perceive to be wrong or unfair on the work unit.

☐   ☐   Many employees believe that it is your job to motivate them and make them happy.

☐   ☐   Many employees seem more concerned about their rights than their responsibilities.

If you answered Yes to any of the statements above, it is important that you reaffirm team goals and move employees' focus off themselves and onto the customer.

Exercise to Inspire Team Purpose:

What Do We Stand For?

The following exercise facilitates employees' understanding and their ownership of work unit goals. It focuses on what the team should Stand For, those non-negotiable conditions of employment.

STEP ONE:

Ask employees: "What are three things we want to be known for, stake our reputation on and never compromise regardless of circumstance?"

For example, Walt Disney built a worldwide dynasty based on three simple Stand Fors:

- Wholesome family entertainment

- Outstanding guest relations

- State-of-the-art/cutting-edge visual effects

Ray Kroc, founder of McDonald's, probably knew that the restaurant chain wouldn't be all things to all people or compete with other restaurants on the basis of ambiance or physical comfort. But he was determined that his restaurants would excel at being:

- Fast

- Clean

- Consistent (from one property to another)

- Affordable (provide a tasty product at a very competitive price)

STEP TWO:

Have each employee write down three work unit Stand Fors. Ask them to keep their responses simple. You're not asking them to develop a mission statement. You just want them to identify what should be the focus of their attention.

Examples of Stand Fors that are frequently nominated include (not in any order of importance):

- Technical/clinical competence

- Service quality

- Teamwork

- Fiscal prudence

- Safety

- Cleanliness

- Efficiency

- Professional development

Have employees share their proposed Stand Fors. Many of the responses will be very similar but worded differently. Therefore, the group organizes the input into similar categories and decides on the top three Stand Fors.

STEP THREE:

With employee input, convert the Stand Fors into best practices. Be specific and concise: What will employees say and do to demonstrate their commitment to each Stand For? Consider the following examples:

Customer Service

Ask employees to identify their customers (both internal and external). Focusing on one customer at a time, ask:

- What are their needs and expectations?

- Which of our services do they value most?

- What are the criteria by which they evaluate our services?

Ask employees to develop a comprehensive list of Best Customer Service Practices.

Potential responses may include:

- When we meet a customer for the first time, we introduce ourselves by name and position.

- We are mindful of our nonverbal communication. We establish eye contact, smile and provide the customer our undivided attention.

- Before we terminate a discussion with a customer, we ask: "Is there anything else I can do for you? Do you have any other questions that I can answer?"

- When we answer the telephone, we say:

  - "Good morning (afternoon or evening). This is the_____department. How may I help you?" We attempt to answer the phone within three rings. All employees pick up the phone if they are in a position to do so. We put a smile in our voice.

- Under no conditions do we disagree with one another in eyesight or earshot of the customer.

Teamwork

Ask employees the following questions:

- In what ways are we customers to one another?

- Which groups within our work unit are interdependent on one another?

- Are they meeting each other's needs and expectations?

- What is the impact on the customer if we don't cooperate within and between shifts, work units and job classifications?

Ask employees to provide a comprehensive list of Best Teamwork Practices. Potential responses may include:

- We make offers of assistance to co-workers without being asked.

- We ask for help and don't expect people to read our minds.

- We don't leave the work unit for extended periods of time without informing someone.

- We don't read a newspaper or get involved in personal phone conversations on paid, productive work time.

- When in conflict with a team member, we talk to the person behind closed doors in a direct, honest and respectful manner. If necessary, we agree to disagree and decide how this unresolved conflict should be handled. Gossiping and tattling is not tolerated.

Professional Development

Ask employees the following questions related to professional development:

- Why is it critical to remain cutting-edge and state-of-the-art in your field?

- Regardless of position, does the need to grow professionally ever end?

- In what ways is it a shared responsibility between the organization and you to continuously develop your knowledge and skills?

- Do you agree that it is the leader's job to create a learning culture within the work unit? What would that look like?

Ask employees to develop a comprehensive list of Best Practices for Professional Development. Potential responses may include:

- We seek opportunities for continuous learning as indicated by...

- We are open to new ideas and flexible about changes that impact our practice as indicated by...

- We offer whatever assistance is necessary to facilitate a new employee's development as indicated by...

- We join professional associations and read journals to remain state-of-the-art and cutting-edge in our profession.

STEP FOUR:

Once a complete list of Best Practices for each Stand For is developed:

- Have employees sign off on them indicating that they understand these to be standards of conduct for which everyone will be held accountable.

- Facilitate a discussion on how employees should provide feedback to one another in a direct and respectful manner when someone slips up on one of the commitments.

- Integrate the Stand Fors with accompanying Best Practices into the employee performance appraisal process.

- Develop a user-friendly method to determine if employees are adhering to the Best Practices.

- Provide regular performance feedback throughout the year to ensure that there are no surprises or new issues raised for an employee during the annual evaluation.

Discussion Questions

Are your employees focused on work unit goals, or are they primarily motivated by individual self-interests?

_____

_____

_____

_____

What can you do to keep employees constantly aware of and sensitive to the work unit's mission and values?

_____

_____

_____

_____

Has your work unit developed a set of Stand Fors? Have your Stand Fors been converted into Best Practices?

_____

_____

_____

_____

God grant me the serenity
to accept the things I cannot change,
the courage to change the things I can,
and the wisdom to know the difference.

The Serenity Prayer

SEPARATE PROBLEMS FROM REALITIES

There is no problem so difficult that it can't be solved. If it can't be solved, it's not a problem. It's a reality. You must accept realities and solve the problems that come with them.

A problem is an obstacle to employees' success or satisfaction that is within your sphere of influence to overcome. A reality is an obstacle that is outside your control. You don't have the necessary authority, resources, autonomy or influence to make the desired change.

You have a real dilemma on your hands when employees believe that a specific obstacle is a problem when you know it to be a reality. If employees believe an improvement in working conditions will or should happen, they begin to feel entitled to the thing they want, and they will blame you if they don't get it. Also, when employees assume that if they complain enough something positive will happen, they become consumed with self-righteous indignation when their desires go unmet.

Ironically, when employees dwell on the negative, they make themselves even less happy. This is because what you focus on you get more of. Employees especially undermine their job satisfaction when they constantly complain about everyday work frustrations and take for granted the positive aspects of the job. Ungrateful people can't be happy.

How to Address Employee Negativity

To reduce the amount of complaining on your work unit, consider engaging in the following leadership activities:

- Help employees separate problems from realities.

- Encourage them to focus on those problems that can be independently solved within the work team.

- Educate them on how to accept and adjust to those everyday work frustrations that are outside anyone's ability to overcome.

- Don't tolerate or reinforce griping and dumping, whining and pouting.

- Teach employees problem solving and conflict resolution skills so that you're not placed in the middle of every co-worker dispute.

- Reinforce the concept of personal responsibility. Despite the inherent irritations within the work environment, hold employees accountable for a positive attitude, a strong work ethic and a constructive response to stressful situations.

Three Levels of Control

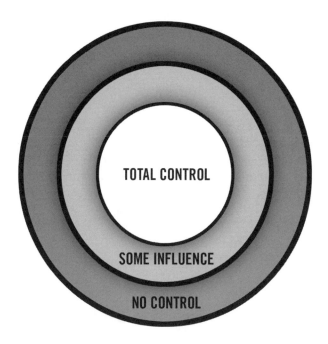

Before attempting to remove obstacles to success, it is important that you identify up front how much actual control you have to effectively address the issue. Listed below are three levels of control beginning with the least amount of influence.

Level One: No Control to Overcome Obstacles

This level encompasses the things that employees worry or complain about but are largely powerless to do anything to alleviate. Examples may include:

- Overall health of the economy

- Industry trends

- Financial well-being of your organization

- Organizational structure

- Executive team's leadership style/quality of decisions

- Organizational priorities

If employees constantly complain about obstacles to success that are outside their control to overcome, they begin to feel powerless and view themselves as victims. To make matters worse, by constantly complaining, employees have less psychic energy to act affirmatively on those obstacles that *are* within their control.

Level Two: Some Influence to Overcome Obstacles

This level of control encompasses those areas in which employees can actually make a difference, but the outcome is dependent on the cooperation of people outside the team. Therefore, employees must be prepared to deal in good faith with these individuals who have their own self-interests, priorities and perspectives. You can facilitate employees' success operating on this level of control by engaging in the following activities:

- Conduct team building workshops between interdependent work units where employees share their needs and expectations of one another and then negotiate commitments for behavior change that will make each other's jobs more satisfying and effective.

- Share relevant information with your employees so that they see the big picture and understand the context in which they are performing their job.

- Help employees understand how their actions have a direct impact on others.

Level Three: Total Control to Overcome Obstacles

This level represents the most effective use of employees' time, because the team does not need permissions and resources from someone else to solve its problems. Obstacles to job success are totally within the work unit's control to overcome.

Within this context, employees' primary focus is on their own conduct and on setting goals that are within their reach. Of course, employees should be concerned about how other work units are performing their jobs. But the focus should be on "getting our own house in order" before we point the finger of blame at someone else.

Problems versus Reality Exercise

The following is a practical exercise to help employees separate problems from realities. It also helps employees maintain realistic expectations of what you can do to facilitate their job success.

STEP ONE:

Engage in an Appreciative Inquiry Session

Employees brainstorm everything that they enjoy about the nature, function and scope of their job including:

- Resources that exist to facilitate their success.

- Positive relationships with co-workers and customers.

- The organization's mission and values.

Have employees cite examples of when the team exceeded a customer's expectations or exhibited outstanding teamwork in response to a challenging situation.

STEP TWO:

Identify Work Frustrations

Employees brainstorm obstacles that serve as an impediment to producing a high quality product or service. Don't ask employees to identify obstacles to their job satisfaction, because their top priority on the job is not to be happy—it is to be successful. Happiness on the job is a byproduct of success. It comes from taking pride in one's work and seeing the positive results of one's efforts.

STEP THREE:

Separate Problems from Realities

Participants decide whether each identified obstacle to success is a problem or a reality. It's a problem if the obstacle is within the work unit's total control to overcome. It's a reality if the obstacle is a frustration inherent in the work environment or if the team can't independently make the frustration go away.

Realities may include:

- Financial constraints

- Customer-staff ratios

- Space limitations

- Documentation responsibilities

- Insurance/government reimbursement processes

STEP FOUR:

Choose Which Problems to Solve

Employees choose the top three problems to work on based on the following criteria:

- The payoff for solving this problem is significant.

- The success probability is high.

- The degree of effort is reasonable.

STEP FIVE:

Determine How the Problem Will Be Solved

Employees advance solutions, identify action steps to be taken, assign roles and responsibilities, develop criteria for measuring success and agree on monitoring and evaluation strategies.

STEP SIX:

Discuss How to Handle Realities

The leader facilitates a work unit discussion on how to best address identified realities. Issues to be addressed include how employees can effectively:

- Accept and adjust to frustrations outside their control.

- Stop focusing on the negative aspects of the work environment.

- Reduce the amount of complaining.

- Acknowledge and appreciate what is good and right within the work unit.

Solving problems that are within employees' control takes courage, determination, patience and persistence. And while employees can't overcome all obstacles, they can choose not to be inordinately jostled about by them. Successfully adapting to the inherent limitations in their work is an act of maturity. Without this ability, employees take premature stands, play the roles of victim or martyr and set themselves up for more frustration.

Discussion Questions

Do your employees focus on frustrations that are outside their control? Please explain.

_____

_____

_____

_____

_____

_____

How do you plan to reach a common understanding of what can or cannot be solved?

_____

_____

_____

_____

_____

_____

Do you have an effective process in place to solve problems that are within your control? Please describe.

_____

_____

_____

_____

_____

_____

Do your employees know the difference between griping and dumping and actually taking responsibility for solving problems that they identify? Please describe.

_____

_____

_____

_____

_____

_____

_____

Man created language to satisfy his
deep need to complain.

Lily Tomlin

9

CONFIRM YOUR DECISION MAKING AUTHORITY

Have you ever participated in a lengthy problem solving process assuming that you had the final authority to make a decision, and then discover that you were only serving in an advisory capacity? Then to add insult to injury, your group's recommendations got rejected. Naturally, you would feel undermined and reluctant to participate in future endeavors.

To avoid such an occurrence, it is important that you clarify roles at the onset of any deliberative process. Specifically, the following questions need to be answered:

Who is the final **Decision Maker**? This person(s) has authority to approve the decision and give the green light for it to be implemented.

Who is the **Coordinator** of the decision making process? The coordinator(s) selects participants to be involved in the deliberations, conducts the meetings and ensures that the group achieves its stated objectives. The decision maker and the coordinator are not always the same person.

Who are the **Meeting Participants**? These are the individuals who are directly involved in the decision making process. They are being utilized on a consultative basis to recommend a course of action. (Meeting participants can be the decision makers as in self-directed work teams and management-employee partnership models.)

Are there additional **Stakeholders**? Stakeholders have a vested interest in the final decision but are not directly involved in the deliberative process. It should be decided up front how and when these individuals will be given an opportunity for input or at least be kept in the loop. For example:

- Will they be informed of the decision making process from the beginning?

- Will they be provided periodic status reports throughout the decision making process?

- Should we provide an "open comments" period in which they are given an opportunity for input before any decision is made?

- Will they be informed of the decision after it is made but before its implementation?

- How will the decision be explained?

- Will they have a say about how to implement the decision?

In certain circumstances, you may determine that specific individuals should **not** be informed of a decision until it is implemented. When this is the case, develop strategies to ensure confidentiality throughout the deliberative process. Explain to all participants the consequences for a breach of trust. Determine in advance how to respond to a direct question from outsiders regarding the deliberations.

Problem Solving Steps

Listed below are specific problem solving steps along with critical issues that must be addressed to make effective decisions.

Problem Diagnoses:

The full nature and scope of a problem must be thoroughly examined before solutions are advanced. The most important issues that need to be addressed include:

- What are the symptoms of the problem to be solved?

- What are the root causes of the problem?

- How serious is the problem? What's the driving force or compelling reason to solve it?

- What would be the negative outcomes if we don't make a change?

- What will success look like if we solve the problem? Will results be quantifiable? (If not, the improved future state must be verifiable in some way.)

- What is currently working? (Appreciate the positive aspects of the status quo while you examine ways to improve it. You don't want to throw the baby out with the bathwater.)

Consideration of Solutions:

Establish criteria for choosing the best solution:

- Is the solution practical?

- Is the success probability high?

- Is the degree of effort reasonable?

- Is it cost effective?

- Is it time sensitive?

- Do solutions under consideration address the root causes of the problem?

- Before we make a decision, have we examined all available solutions to this problem?

- Could this solution solve one problem but create new ones? What might be the unintended consequences of our decision?

- Have we taken into consideration all the stakeholders who will be impacted by this change?

Post-decision Activities:

Design an infrastructure to support the change:

- Are new systems and processes indicated?

- Are changes in reporting relationships necessary?

- What resources are necessary for successful implementation?

- Are there new outcomes to measure?

- Have we locked in methods and timetables for implementation including the assignment of roles and responsibilities?

- Are the deadlines realistic?

- Have we considered the amount of change that people can effectively accommodate given their everyday responsibilities?

- Have we considered the knowledge and skills of employees to implement the change?

- Have we considered the consequences for individuals who don't follow through on assigned tasks?

- How will we monitor and evaluate outcomes?

Selling the Solution:

It is the responsibility of the change agent to answer the following questions:

- Why is the status quo unacceptable?

- What are the advantages of the change?

- What do customers and employees stand to gain by the change?

- How will we relate the change to the organization's and/or work unit's mission, vision and values?

- Have we anticipated and planned for ambivalence or resistance to the decision?

- Who will likely object to the change?

- What questions or concerns are likely to be raised?

- How will we effectively respond to these concerns?

- How will we demonstrate that our solution meets their perceived needs and expectations?

- Should we explain alternative courses of action that were considered and why they were rejected?

- Should we share some of the difficulties we had in making the decision?

- Should we explain why certain people were included in and/or excluded from the deliberative process?

- Have we communicated specifically how each person or group can contribute to the success of the change?

Common Concerns about Change:

Plan your responses to the following potential objections:

- "We have always done it this way. It's working and we're satisfied. Why fix something that's not broken?"

- "Why now?"

- "How do you know this will make things better?"

- "Has it worked any place else?"

- "This represents more work. We're already overloaded. We don't have the time to do this."

- "What new things will we have to learn? How much time will we have to learn this?"

- "I won't mind this change, but others won't accept it. It's going to make a lot of people unhappy."

- "We're different and/or special. This should not apply to us."

- "Are you open to better ideas?"

- "Will we have a say in how and/or when this will be implemented?"

Consider the Advantages of a Task Force versus a Committee

All too frequently, committees take on a life of their own and lose a sense of purpose and urgency. Discussions become theoretical and esoteric. They become a forum for lengthy debates and grandstanding. All too often, committee meetings do not achieve any measurable results. Participants begin to wonder if this is the best use of their time.

On the other hand, task forces are formed to focus on a specific problem. They are solution-oriented and have a bias toward action. Sometimes, task force participants set a deadline to meet their objective. They treat this time frame as an outside limit. On rare occasions when an unanticipated obstacle presents itself, participants decide to extend the project for another couple of weeks. But that's it.

Once they accomplish the objective, the task force adjourns. Members of a task force are usually energized because they are associated with concrete, positive change. They add speed and efficiency to the organizational development process.

Discussion Questions

Have you ever been involved in a lengthy deliberative process, believing that you had decision making authority only to find out later that you were serving in an advisory capacity? How did it make you feel?

_____

_____

_____

_____

_____

_____

Are there any decisions your organization or work unit is about to make in which there is a lack of clarity regarding the roles and authority of participants in the problem solving process? What can you do to help clarify individual roles?

_____

_____

_____

_____

_____

_____

Think of a decision that was made within your organization or work unit that didn't work out. Was the decision flawed? Did the implementation of the decision break down? Was there poor communication with stakeholders not directly involved in the decision making process? What other factors may have been involved?

_____

_____

_____

_____

_____

_____

Do you have committees within your organization that have lost their way? What can you do to get them back on track?

_____

_____

_____

_____

_____

_____

Once you make a decision, the universe conspires to make it happen.

Ralph Waldo Emerson

LEAD EFFECTIVE MEETINGS

Throughout the course of a week, you are probably expected to attend numerous management meetings and participate on various committees. All of these meetings make it exceedingly difficult to address the pressing needs of your work unit in a timely manner. After meetings adjourn you have to play "catch up;" responding to e-mail messages and phone calls, completing time-sensitive administrative tasks, and addressing employee and customer relations issues.

You probably would not mind attending meetings if they were efficiently run and produced timely concrete results. All too often, however, these meetings:

- Start late/don't end on time.

- Drag on and lose focus.

- Feel like a slow moving soap opera. (You can be absent for three or four meetings only to discover that you didn't miss a thing—the same issues come up again and again without closure).

- Become debating forums.

- Provide an opportunity for grandstanding and ego-tripping. (One person dominates the discussion; lecturing or talking over others. There is no free flowing dialogue or balance in participation.)

- Become nothing more than the leader making a series of announcements. (People wonder, "Why have meetings when e-mail would suffice?")

- Lack clarity on how decisions will be implemented. Results are compromised when no person or group is accountable for outcomes.

- Include participants who have no vested interest in the topics discussed or they lack enough information to contribute.

- Include participants who don't pay attention. (Texting, accepting phone calls, engaging in side conversation.)

- Include participants who complain about realities that cannot be changed.

- Include participants who spend time blaming others instead of focusing on what needs to be changed in them.

Conduct a Meeting Audit to Ensure Productive Meetings

To avoid wasting time participating in dysfunctional meetings, conduct a meeting audit in which you reach agreement on answers to the following questions.

Meeting Purpose and Context

- Do participants understand the reason for the team's existence?

- How does the team relate to the larger organization in terms of role, scope of responsibilities and level of authority?

- Do participants have enough expertise and information to make high quality decisions?

- Are agendas developed and forwarded to participants before meetings begin?

- Do participants have an opportunity to add items to the agenda before or at the beginning of meetings?

- At the onset of meetings, do participants discuss what they want to accomplish?

- At the end of each meeting do participants have an opportunity to evaluate the quality of the interaction and whether the identified objectives were met?

Planning and Logistics:

- How often should we meet?

- When should we meet (best day and time)?

- How long should we meet?

- Where should we meet?

- Who should attend?

- Who should facilitate meetings? When that person can't attend, who will be the leader?

- Who will take minutes? How and when will the minutes be distributed and verified for accuracy?

- Are records of the last discussion available before the next meeting begins?

- When a decision is made, do we build in implementation steps as appropriate?

- How should we deal with participants who miss meetings, come late, leave early, drift in and out or multitask?

Confidentiality and Trust:

- What topics for discussion are confidential?

- What are the consequences for leaking confidential information, misrepresenting the team discussion or bad-mouthing individual team members to outsiders?

- How and when should we share specific information regarding decisions that we make? Do we need to anticipate and plan for resistance to our decisions? How can we best package our decisions to get people's understanding and buy-in?

- Are participants willing to make sacrifices on behalf of the team? Are they engaged? If not, should they continue to be members of the team?

Interactions:

- Is there a balance of participation at our meetings, or do a few individuals dominate the discussion?

- Do participants shy away from controversial issues and play it safe?

- Can participants play the role of devil's advocate without fear of retaliation? Are contrary positions encouraged?

- Are ideas shared without fear of ridicule?

- Are ideas ignored or prematurely discredited?

- Do we recognize and use the strengths and abilities of each team member?

- How well do we manage conflict? Are we direct, honest and respectful to one another?

- In discussing a difficult issue, do we draw out multiple alternatives, challenge assumptions and provide objective facts to work with?

- Do we get caught up in "analysis paralysis," or do we make timely decisions with the best information available?

- Are decisions made in haste? Or does it seem to take forever to get closure on issues?

- Do side conversations constantly break out?

- Do we easily get sidetracked?

- Are meetings structured, organized and efficient?

Leadership:

- Does the leader demonstrate effective meeting management skills?

- Is the leader goal-focused and results-oriented?

- Does the leader ensure that participants' feelings and opinions are heard, understood and respected?

- Is the leader perceived to be fair and objective, without any hidden agenda?

- Is the leader credible and an effective spokesperson for the team within the organization?

Common Meeting Problems and How to Deal with Them

Listed below are some of the most common examples of meeting dysfunction along with solutions to use when they surface.

Problem:

Participants are confused about a specific meeting's objectives. The discussions are unfocused.

Solution:

Have an agenda for each meeting. Allow participants an opportunity to shape the agenda. Articulate a set of objectives at the beginning of each meeting. At the conclusion of the meeting, ask participants:

- "Did we accomplish what we set out to do?"

- "What did you like about this meeting?"

- "What could we have done better?"

Problem:

Meetings start late.

Solution:

Participants should reach a consensus on a minimum acceptable number of people it takes to start a meeting. If that number is not reached within ten minutes of the meeting's start time, adjourn the session.

Problem:

Meetings don't end on time.

Solution:

The team should agree on the ideal length of meetings and then stick to it. Set realistic agendas. It is better to discuss a few issues in a thorough manner than to try to rush through too many.

Problem:

We have too many meetings.

Solution:

Address the following questions:

- "Would anyone notice or care if we held fewer meetings or stopped meeting altogether?"

- "Does everyone need to participate at each meeting?"

- "Is there a better format to address these issues?"

- "Instead of meeting, could one person with the expertise or vested interest investigate the problem and recommend a course of action?"

Consider a rule that if enough people can't attend a meeting, it gets canceled. If meetings get canceled regularly, you must evaluate the issue of purpose and commitment.

Problem:

Participants don't follow through on decisions that are made. The team can't seem to get closure on issues.

Solution:

Whenever appropriate, develop methods and timetables for implementing decisions. Identify roles and responsibilities, and develop a monitoring strategy to track results.

Problem:

The same one or two people who come in late expect a summary on what was decided or want the group to reconsider its decision.

Solution:

Do not accommodate them. In particular, don't revisit decisions because missing participants later declare that they are not in agreement with the team's conclusions.

Problem:

One or two people dominate the meeting. There is no balance of participation.

Solution:

Designate a facilitator (other than the meeting leader) to monitor the group interaction and remind participants to be sensitive to the inclusion needs of others:

- "John, thank you for your thoughts. Now let's consider what others have to say on this issue."

- "We have not yet heard from everyone. Who else has something to say?"

- "Sally, it looks as if you have been trying to get in on this discussion. Please share your thoughts."

- "I don't believe Steve was finished talking yet. Please don't interrupt. Steve, please continue."

Problem:

Meetings drag on.

Solution:

- "It appears that we're getting off the track. Can we come back to the issue at hand?"

- "We've spent a great deal of time on this one issue, and we only have 30 minutes left to discuss the other agenda items. How should we handle this?"

Problem:

Decisions are made hastily.

Solution:

"This decision will have a significant impact on the organization. Do you think we've given it enough serious consideration? Perhaps we should think about it some more, get additional information or secure input from others before we decide."

Problem:

Counterproductive and dysfunctional communication permeates the discussion. For example, some participants exhibit passive-aggressive behavior.

Solution:

"Jane, you look upset. You're rolling your eyes (folding your arms, having side conversations with people around you, smirking when someone makes a comment, etc.). Would you like to share your thoughts with the group?"

The leader should consider coaching this person immediately following the meeting (or before the next meeting). Describe the person's behavior with specific expectations for positive change. Consequences for continued counterproductive conduct should also be discussed. The team might want to consider developing meeting guidelines that describe what constructive participation looks like and specific behaviors that should be avoided.

Problem:

Participants are playing it safe. They are conflict averse.

Solution:

Never penalize participants for sharing their feelings or beliefs, providing they package their ideas in a constructive and collaborative manner. Encourage participants to play the role of devil's advocate. Convene a special meeting for participants to review assertiveness, conflict management and problem solving skills.

What Makes an Effective Team?

The following statements describe the characteristics of an effective work team. First, rank order the four statements that you believe are the **most important characteristics** of a well-functioning group.

Next, rank order the four statements that you believe are the **least important characteristics** of a well-functioning group. When you are finished, compare the results with members of your team and explain the reasons for your ranking.

- The objectives of the work team are explicitly formulated with accompanying monitoring and evaluation systems in place to ensure positive outcomes.

- Team members give and receive feedback to one another in a direct and honest fashion.

- The leader expects continuous improvement in work quality, technical competence and customer service.

- Team members are included in decision making processes that directly influence their work. Employees are listened to when changes are considered.

- Leaders know what they Stand For and will never compromise regardless of circumstance. Team mission, vision and values have been clearly established and communicated.

- There exists a retribution-free communication environment where members feel free to play the role of devil's advocate without fear of retaliation.

- An agenda is provided for all team meetings. People stay on track, methods and timetables are developed to ensure follow-through on decisions made and results are evaluated.

- Team members' job satisfaction is seriously considered in all management decisions. Leaders are held accountable for positive employee relations.

- Team members are assigned specific responsibilities and are held accountable for positive outcomes.

- Information is freely shared among team members. Top-down, bottom-up and lateral communication is encouraged. There is relative transparency in decision making processes.

- Performance standards, policies, procedures, guidelines and protocols have been established. People are held accountable for adhering to them.

- Team members are recognized for their contributions. People feel appreciated.

Discussion Questions

How are participants clear about the objectives of your meetings?

Describe the quality of group interactions?

What guidelines for conduct should be established to ensure productive meetings?

How do you address problems with follow-through and achieving closure on the decisions you make?

Teamwork is the ability to work together
toward a common vision;
the ability to direct individual accomplishment
toward organizational objectives.
It is the fuel that allows common people
to attain uncommon results.

Andrew Carnegie

11

FACILITATE COLLABORATIVE RELATIONSHIPS

Sometimes employee personality conflicts and work style differences make it difficult to achieve work unit goals. Listed below are a few indicators of communication dysfunction. Use it as a check list. Do your employees conduct themselves in the following manner?

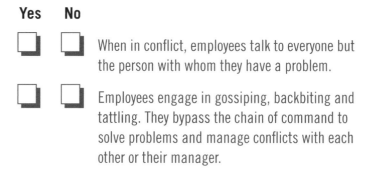

Yes   No

☐   ☐   When in conflict, employees talk to everyone but the person with whom they have a problem.

☐   ☐   Employees engage in gossiping, backbiting and tattling. They bypass the chain of command to solve problems and manage conflicts with each other or their manager.

☐ ☐ Bullies and passive-aggressive behavior are tolerated on the work unit. Employees lack the skill or courage to set limits with co-workers who display disruptive behaviors.

☐ ☐ Employees rarely give each other the benefit of the doubt. When something goes wrong, employees automatically assign malicious intent, finger point and scapegoat.

If the answer is Yes to any of the statements above, consider engaging in the following exercises.

An Exercise to Identify Best and Worst Communication Practices

"What does it look like to practice effective communication within our work unit?" If you ask employees this question, you may get a variety of divergent responses. This exercise is designed to help employees identify the work unit's standards of conduct to which everyone should be held accountable.

STEP ONE:

Have employees brainstorm behavioral characteristics of the "Co-Worker from Hell." (These are the behaviors that should not be tolerated on the work unit.)

STEP TWO:

Have employees name past or present co-workers who serve as role models for outstanding work unit communications. Next, they list specific behaviors that these role models demonstrate on a consistent basis. By so doing, employees are developing a list of best communication practices to which everyone should be held accountable.

STEP THREE:

Have employees adopt the "Best and Worst Communication Practices" as a social contract: "These are the behaviors we expect of one another, and these are the behaviors that should not be tolerated on our unit." Each employee signs off on the contract, which is placed in the employee's file. The best and worst practices list can also be used as criteria for evaluating employees during the annual performance appraisal.

Exercise to Develop Best Conflict Management Practices

STEP ONE:

Share with employees four possible types of responses to conflict:

Aggressive Responses:

- Shouting, swearing, threatening

- Pounding table, slamming doors or drawers, throwing objects

- Offensive hand gestures

- Violating others' personal space

- Public criticism

- Interrupting

- Negatively loaded words (e.g. incompetent, lazy)

- Cultural or gender slurs

Passive-aggressive Responses:

- Gossiping, tattling

- Silent treatment

- Short, sarcastic responses

- Complaining before and after meetings but refusing to attend or participate during meetings

- Helping and/or communicating with only those co-workers they personally like

- Refusing to state what they are upset about—expecting others to read their minds

- Nonverbal behaviors: sighing, eye-rolling, frowning, sneering, muttering, avoiding eye contact

- Constant griping or whining, negative statements such as, "This will never work." "Nobody ever listens to us." "It's not my job."

- Exaggerating problems

- Apologizing for disruptive behavior but continuing the behavior

Passive Responses:

- Avoiding confrontation

- Allowing abusive behavior to continue by not setting limits

- Saying Yes when No is meant

- Apologizing even when nothing was done wrong

- Asking for permission when authority is already given

- Making excuses for not speaking up: "It will only make things worse." "It won't do any good." "Someone's feelings might get hurt." "The person will retaliate." "I might look foolish."

Assertive Responses:

- Asking for what is wanted in a direct, honest and respectful manner

- Trying to understand the other person's perspective

- Not ascribing malicious intent

- Not assuming the other person knows how you feel

Assertiveness calls for you to deal with the other person in good faith, and to consider modifying your own behavior, which usually makes it easier for the other person to change in the direction you want. It is a collaborative approach to co-worker conflict geared toward achieving a win-win outcome. The objective is for both parties to have their needs satisfied.

STEP TWO:

Share with employees the following Assertive Fair-Fighting Techniques that lead to healthy co-worker relationships:

- Don't expect perfection from your co-workers. Unrealistic expectations of others are a setup for frustration and self-righteous indignation. Rather than judge others, offer assistance to facilitate their improvement.

- Choose your conflicts carefully. The most credible employees are those who don't often complain. But when they do, others listen because they have earned the right to be heard. Don't make catastrophes out of everyday frustrations. Keep things in perspective.

- Talk directly, honestly and respectfully to the co-worker with whom you are experiencing conflict. Avoid indirect, triangulated and cowardly communication such as gossiping, backbiting and tattling. Always be loyal to those not present.

- Keep your confrontations behind closed doors, outside the public arena. When you criticize someone in full public view of others, you create a spectator sport. The person has little chance to save face and keep self-esteem intact. Wash your dirty linen in private, not in public.

- Talk to the person with whom you are in conflict at the earliest opportunity, providing you are cool, calm and collected. What is said in the heat of frustration might irreparably damage your relationship.

- Be issue-oriented. Avoid using words that elicit defensiveness such as "stupid," "ignorant," "lazy," "incompetent," "disrespectful" or "unprofessional." This kind of feedback is hopelessly general and ambiguous, to say nothing of insulting. It does not tell others what you specifically want them to do differently to better meet your needs.

- Address one issue at a time. Don't sandbag co-workers by privately keeping score of their transgressions. By doing so, you build up animosity, and you are likely to "go off" when you finally confront the person.

- Know when to terminate the conversation if you can't agree. Don't keep repeating yourself with the false hope that the co-worker will finally see it your way. Agree to disagree for the time being.

- Get help from a third party when necessary. Ask this person to coach you on the best way to handle the situation or to mediate the conflict. This person should be someone who is perceived to be objective and not personally involved in the conflict.

- Know when to put the disagreement behind you and start a new day. Keep the lines of communication open. Remember, you don't have to personally like a co-worker to maintain a professional relationship. You can be friendly without being friends.

- In the end, control over anyone else is an illusion. You can't make people conform to your desires. Nor are you responsible for their actions. But even if you are not to blame for the conflict, you can never abdicate responsibility for your reaction to it. If you allow people to control your emotions, you are allowing them to have control over you. Don't allow them to drag you in the mud with their dysfunctional behavior. Always maintain the high ground.

STEP THREE:

Have employees identify three Assertive Fair Fighting Techniques that are frequently violated on the work unit. Ask employees why this happens and what training and development resources they need to become more success-ful at managing conflict.

STEP FOUR:

Have employees adopt these Assertive Fair Fight-ing Techniques as a social contract for the work unit. All employees sign their names to the contract indicating that they will abide by these standards of conduct and will be held accountable for them. Integrate these standards into the performance appraisal process.

Discussion Questions

Do employees understand your role in the conflict management process? Do they think that it is your responsibility to get directly involved in every employee conflict? What will you do to facilitate employee's accepting responsibility for conflicts?

_____

_____

_____

_____

_____

_____

What *is* your role in this process? How do you facilitate direct and respectful communications among employees on your work unit? For example, when employees complain to you about what someone did, do you redirect them back to the person with whom they are having a conflict?

_____

_____

_____

_____

_____

_____

Do your employees need training on how to manage difficult conversations? How do you plan to meet this developmental need?

_____

_____

_____

_____

_____

_____

_____

_____

The way a team plays as a whole determines
its success. You may have the greatest bunch of
individual stars in the world, but if they don't play
together, the club won't be worth a dime.

Babe Ruth

NEGOTIATE WORK
UNIT ROLES

Roger Harrison, an organizational behavior specialist, describes role negotiation as "the process that involves changing through negotiation with other interested parties the role that an individual or group performs in the organization… which activity he is supposed to perform, what decisions he can make, to whom he reports…"

The role negotiation process is valuable because it avoids probing into an employee's personal feelings toward the manager or co-workers. Instead, the focus is on exploring observable behaviors that impact work unit functioning.

The process is particularly useful for identifying issues of communication among interdependent groups. It provides an opportunity for participants to make commitments for positive change that will set each other up for success and make each other look good in the eyes of the customer.

Indicators of Intergroup Conflict

Listed below are characteristics of interdependent work units that are in a state of perpetual conflict. There is distrust, polarization and a breakdown of communication between them. Use this as a check-list. Can you identify two or more interdependent groups that are working at cross purposes with one another?

Yes **No**

☐ ☐ One group feels it gets little or no respect from the other.

☐ ☐ One group feels that the other gets preferential treatment from their manager.

☐ ☐ One group feels it works much harder than the other.

☐ ☐ One group feels that the other has mostly incompetent people working in it.

☐ ☐ One group feels it gets much less recognition than the other.

☐ ☐ One group acts as if it is superior to the other.

☐ ☐ Individuals from one group regularly talk about the other in a snide, cynical and sarcastic manner. There is plenty of gossiping, bad-mouthing and tattling.

☐ ☐ Conflicts between the groups are swept under the carpet. People are unwilling to talk to each other.

Yes **No**

☐ ☐ Pertinent information or knowledge is withheld from the groups.

☐ ☐ The groups constantly bicker and quarrel over trivial issues.

☐ ☐ Managers are in open conflict with each other. They avoid each other, or use their groups as a sounding board to criticize each other.

☐ ☐ There is a culture of secrecy between the groups. Certain topics can't be discussed in front of members of the other group.

☐ ☐ There is duplication of work.

☐ ☐ There is an abundance of finger pointing when something goes wrong.

☐ ☐ There is a feeling of distrust bordering on paranoia between groups.

If any of these indicators of intergroup conflict apply to your work teams, consider utilizing one of the exercises described in this chapter.

The following exercises are specifically designed to improve the overall quality of relationships between manager and employees, within and between interdependent shifts, job classifications and work units.

Show and Tell Exercise

Bring both groups together and have them take turns sharing with one another the following information. Allow plenty of time for dialogue. In fact, it may take several meetings to effectively address these issues, but it's time well spent.

- A summary of our job descriptions

- The goals of our group

- The customers we serve

- What a typical day looks like

- Aspects of the job we find most/least rewarding

- Some of our constraints and limitations and how we overcome these obstacles

- How our two groups are interdependent

- Areas of role ambiguity that have led to conflict between our two groups

- Ways to anticipate, plan for or prevent future conflict

- The best way to manage conflict when it occurs in the future

- Ideas for improving communication and cooperation between our groups

- How we can utilize each other's resources to the fullest advantage

- Commitments for positive behavior change to make each other's job more satisfying and effective

Talent/Resource Identification Exercise

It is always a good idea for two interdependent groups to get to know one another on an informal as well as a professional basis. Good relationships grease the results channels. This exercise allows employees to become more knowledgeable about the resources that exist within each group and provides an opportunity to learn from one another. They are less likely to blame one another when something goes wrong if they are sensitive to each other's constraints and limitations.

STEP ONE:

Get to Know One Another

- As an ice breaker, employees share personal activities in which they are engaged that few co-workers know about, such as hobbies, travels, family information or unusual experiences.

- Employees take turns sharing with one another their knowledge and skill sets that could be better utilized by the team(s).

STEP TWO:

Learn From One Another

- Employees arrange a time to teach one another their specific areas of expertise.

- Employees can also decide to "shadow" someone from another shift, job or work unit to observe first-hand the complexities of the person's job.

STEP THREE:

- Periodically, employees take turns publicly recognizing each other for the valuable contributions they make on behalf of the team. They focus on situations in which individuals have demonstrated effective teamwork, communication or customer service.

Work Unit Empathy Exercise

This exercise does not require intergroup dialogue to achieve positive outcomes. In fact, it is sometimes desirable for interdependent groups **not** to get together until each is willing to see the world from the other's perspective.

STEP ONE:

Ask employees to place themselves in the other group's shoes by answering the following questions:

- What specifically does the other group want, need and expect of us?

- Which of these expectations would they say we consistently meet?

- Which expectations would they say we do not consistently meet?

- Are these unmet expectations job-related? Are they reasonable? Do we have the resources to meet these unmet expectations?

- What commitments for positive change are we willing and able to make to facilitate their success?

- Should we meet with this group to share our assessment and offer our commitments for positive change?

- Are we open to their feedback? Will we get defensive if they say something that we don't want to hear?

- What do we want from them to make our job easier, more satisfying and effective?

STEP TWO:

Convene a meeting with the other group to offer commitments for positive change that will facilitate their job success and satisfaction.

Use the following role negotiation process to facilitate a structured dialogue resulting in improved communication between groups.

Intergroup Role Negotiation Exercise

This exercise is designed to achieve a win-win outcome in which both groups advance commitments for positive change on behalf of the other to make their jobs more satisfying and successful.

STEP ONE:

Have the two interdependent teams (Group A and Group B) first meet separately to compose a letter to the other group. The letter should consist of three lists:

Thank You List:

"These are the things that you do well on a consistent basis to make our jobs easier, more satisfying and effective. We appreciate that you do these things because…"

Note: It is impossible for the groups to give too many compliments to each other, providing they are sincere and deserved. Also, a group does not have to be perfect in order to receive a compliment on a particular item. If enough people do something that's worthy of praise, include it on the Thank You List. According to behavior modification principles, those behaviors that are reinforced usually get repeated. You run the risk of extinguishing positive behaviors if you don't reinforce them.

Wish List:

"These are our expectations that you do not consistently meet. We believe that these unmet expectations are job-related, reasonable and within your control. Therefore, we request that you consider making the following commitments for change on our behalf. Please start or stop doing the following things…"

Empathy List:

"These are the things we are willing to start or stop doing to make your job easier, more satisfying and more effective. We are very aware of your past complaints and current concerns. We suspect these items are on your Wish List. Therefore, we are proposing the following commitments for positive change on your behalf…"

STEP TWO:

Have the two groups come together. Spokespersons from each group take turns sharing their Thank You Lists.

STEP THREE:

Have Group A's spokesperson presents its Empathy List to Group B. Group B's spokesperson compares Group A's Empathy List with its own Wish List, and responds in one of three ways:

- "Thank you for identifying this as one of our issues. The item is in fact on our Wish List. Let's talk about it."

- "This item is not on our Wish List, but it's a keeper. We would definitely appreciate if you made this change on our behalf."

- "You are being too hard on yourselves. This item is not on our Wish List. It's not a problem. You can cross it off your Empathy List."

Next, the Group B spokesperson shares with Group A the remaining items on the Wish List that need to be addressed: "We would also like you to consider making the following commitments for positive change that were not on your Empathy List."

Now reverse the process; the Group B spokesperson presents its Empathy List to Group A. Group A's spokesperson provides feedback as described above.

Note: It is strongly recommended that each group shares the Empathy List before it shares the Wish List. This pre-emptive approach of admitting your own deficiencies before hearing them from the other group minimizes the defensiveness of both parties.

STEP FOUR:

Have the groups separate to discuss among themselves those commitments for positive change that they are willing and able to make.

STEP FIVE:

Have the groups reconvene to share their commitments with one another. It is important that the commitments be written in a specific and behaviorally precise manner so they can be monitored and evaluated. After the commitments are accepted by both groups, each team develops methods and timetables and identifies roles and responsibilities to ensure effective implementation of the agreed upon changes.

STEP SIX:

The groups convene approximately two to three months later to review the commitments and evaluate the extent to which they have been honored. Commitments are reaffirmed or adjusted as appropriate. The groups celebrate their mutual success. But it is also critical that real consequences are meted out for any employee who lacks the will or skill to honor commitments.

Exercise to Clarify Levels of Authority

To meet work unit goals, employees need a clear understanding of both their individual and team responsibilities.

This requires that reporting relationships and lines of authority are clearly defined. Specifically, employees must know who has a right to tell them what to do and how much freedom they have to take independent action.

For example, how much authority are you willing to grant employees to make decisions and take action without your knowledge or permission? Much depends on the nature of the activity and the amount of confidence you have in employees to independently achieve positive outcomes. Based on these considerations, negotiate with employees the following levels of control (starting with lowest level of employee autonomy).

Level One:

Employees who identify a problem are expected to gather information and ideas. They present their findings to you with the understanding that you will make a decision on what to do and determine implementation steps.

Level Two:

Employees who identify a problem are expected to gather information and ideas. They present their findings to you and propose a course of action. Together, you consider the merits of the employees' recommendations, but you exercise the authority to make the decision on what to do and determine implementation steps.

Level Three:

Employees who identify a problem are expected to gather information and ideas. They present their findings to you and propose a course of action. Together, you consider the merits of the employees' recommendations. The employees make the decision and determine implementation steps. In this model, the employees are not asking for your permission. Their objective is to communicate and clarify intentions and get your input before taking action.

Level Four:

Employees who identify a problem have the freedom to make decisions and implement them without your advance knowledge, input or consent. They inform you **after** implementation in the spirit of open communication.

Level Five:

Employees have absolute control to take action. They do not have to inform you before or after the decision has been made. You have granted them the freedom, independence and autonomy to make judgment calls.

Meet with employees on a proactive basis to identify the various decisions they make throughout the course of a day. Then reach an understanding on how much authority they have for each situation. Employees also need to be reminded that with freedom to act comes responsibility and accountability for positive results.

Clarify Work Unit Policies and Procedures

Work unit policies, procedures, guidelines and protocols provide employees direction on how the unit's and organization's goals are to be accomplished.

Adherence to policies and procedures creates consistency and predictability which lead to work unit efficiency.

Anarchy reigns when employees complete the same tasks based on personal preferences or idiosyncrasies. A reasonable amount of uniformity and standardization is desirable.

Some policies and procedures may be unnecessarily bureaucratic or arbitrary. They're simply not user friendly to employees or customers.

Employees should know that they have the authority to relax a policy if it's in the best interest of a customer. There are good reasons why a particular policy exists, but the policy should not become a substitute for an employee's common sense and good judgment.

Ask employees to answer the following questions to ensure that work unit policies and procedures facilitate employees' success at serving customers.

Policy and Procedure Audit

- Which policies do we frequently violate?

- What is the intent of these policies?

- Why do we frequently violate them? Are they impractical? Do they provoke customer complaints? Are they not enforced? Are there not enough meaningful consequences for violating them?

- If we change the policies, what should replace them?

- Which unit policies should never be relaxed regardless of circumstance?

- How do we effectively respond to people who demand that we violate these policies?

- Which policies should be relaxed and under what circumstances?

- Which policies of ours do other work units not understand or appreciate? Should we consider changing the policies on their behalf? How can we educate them so that they understand why our policies exist?

- What policies of other work units do we not understand or appreciate? What steps can we take to better understand why these policies exist?

Discussion Questions

Do your employees understand their levels of authority to make decisions or initiate action? Do they exercise that authority, or are they playing it safe? Please explain.

_____

_____

_____

Do your employees view one another as internal customers? Please explain.

_____

_____

_____

What have you done to facilitate role clarity and cooperation
within or between work units?

_____

_____

_____

_____

_____

_____

_____

How do you intend to tear down walls and build bridges
between various shifts, job classifications and/or work units?

_____

_____

_____

_____

_____

_____

_____

_____

How do you achieve a healthy balance between holding everyone accountable for adhering to policies and procedures and providing employees the appropriate amount of freedom, independence, autonomy and control over their jobs?

_____

_____

_____

_____

_____

_____

Which of your policies and procedures are most frequently violated? Is it because there are no real consequences for violating them? Or is it because the policies and procedures are not practical and should be changed?

_____

_____

_____

_____

_____

_____

If you would lift me up,
you must be on higher ground.

Ralph Waldo Emerson

RECOGNIZE EMPLOYEE ACHIEVEMENT

Praise given in the right way for the right reasons at the right time may be your most powerful management tool for reinforcing constructive behavior. In fact, it is impossible to give too much positive feedback to employees, providing you are sincere and they deserve it.

When you compliment people for good work, you not only enhance the professional relationship, you also influence their future conduct. That behavior which is reinforced tends to get repeated.

Unfortunately, too many employees are living in a state of psychological deprivation relative to positive feedback. This is because many leaders are quick to criticize yet reluctant to credit. They practice Management by Exception: When employees do a good job, the leader's response is silence. The belief is that:

- "They're adults, not children. I shouldn't have to slobber all over them with praise."

- "If they don't hear from me, they should assume they're doing a good job."

- "They're getting paid to do a good job. Isn't that enough?"

- "If I praise them too frequently, they will only want more money."

But when the same employees make a mistake, the manager's response is to immediately criticize them for their performance deficiency.

The problem with using silence as a reward is that employees will begin to view you as someone to be avoided. They cringe and wonder what they did wrong every time you approach them or ask them into your office. After all, the only time you speak to them is when they make a mistake.

If you want to avoid the Management by Exception syndrome, condition yourself to notice when employees are doing well. It's a matter of selective perception. Make a conscious effort to observe what is good and right within your team.

Even your most difficult employees are probably doing more good than bad. The best chance you have to facilitate positive behavior change is to build on their strengths, not constantly harp on their weaknesses.

Best Recognition Practices

Use the following reinforcement strategies as a checklist to determine if you engage in recognition activities that contribute to a positive work environment.

Yes   No

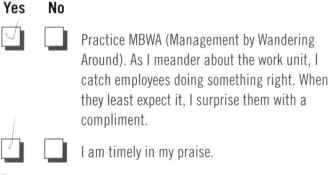 Practice MBWA (Management by Wandering Around). As I meander about the work unit, I catch employees doing something right. When they least expect it, I surprise them with a compliment.

I am timely in my praise.

Comment:

According to feedback experts, the most impact comes from compliments provided as soon as possible after a praiseworthy event.

Yes   No

 I am specific when I praise.

Comment:

As an employee, it is always gratifying to hear from your manager, "You did a nice job on the project," or "I like the way you handled that difficult customer." While this kind of general feedback enhances the personal relationship, it doesn't tell employees what they did to earn your praise. The positive feedback would be more instructive if you said:

- "Thank you for volunteering to lead this project. I really was impressed by how you took everyone's ideas into consideration, investigated all possible solutions to the problem and recommended a viable course of action. And I really appreciated that you met the deadlines that were set for you in advance."

- "You really did a fine job handling that difficult customer. What I liked most is that you patiently listened to his concerns without getting personally defensive, made an apology for the customer's inconvenience even though you were not to blame and successfully negotiated a response that met his expectations."

Yes   No

☐   ☐   I offer pure praise. I don't offer a compliment and then immediately suggest what the employee could have done better: "That was a fine job, but next time I would prefer you..."

Comment

This practice of combining recognition with suggestions for improvement dilutes the positive impact of the compliment. The person is likely to remember only the criticism. If you mix your messages too often, employees will suspect that the only reason you offered the compliment was to get to the criticism.

Yes No

☐ ☐ I encourage co-workers to provide recognition to one another.

Comment:

The responsibility of recognizing good work should not be the leader's alone. Create an environment in which everyone is looking for opportunities to say "Thank you," "Good job" or "I really appreciated when you..."

Yes No

☐ ☐ I publicly recognize employees for their exemplary behavior.

Comment:

Some people get embarrassed by public praise, and sometimes they are resented by other members of the team. So know your employees and team culture before you engage in this form of recognition.

Yes No

☐ ☐ I celebrate team accomplishments. I recognize the efforts of two or more employees who demonstrate effective teamwork on behalf of customers. I don't miss opportunities to reinforce cooperation within and between job classifications, shifts and work units.

☐ ☐ I take a few minutes at the end of the day to send out personalized thank you notes to deserving employees.

Yes   No

☐ ☐   I write up employees who:

- Exceed customer or co-worker expectations.

- Advance an idea that improves the quality of performance, or morale on the work unit.

- Identify a way to make or save money for the organization or work unit.

- Suggest new systems or processes that make the work unit more efficient, safe, clean, error-proof, etc.

Comment:

When providing a copy of the write up, consider asking your manager to send a personalized note on behalf of the division or organization. In addition, forward a copy to the Human Resources Department for the employer's personnel file.

Yes   No

☐ ☐   I celebrate special occasions such as employment anniversaries, promotions, new hires, retirements, birthdays, returns from maternity leave and professional recognition weeks.

☐ ☐   I give out flowers, candy, gift certificates for movies, spas, dinners and sporting events.

☐ ☐   I order lunch from a local deli or pizza parlor. I have employees bring in their favorite dishes or organize a "potluck."

Comment:

Food is always a good motivator. A team that breaks bread together stays together.

Yes   No

☐   ☐   I reward employees who have perfect attendance (no unscheduled absences or tardiness in a calendar year) and outstanding attendance (two or fewer absences or occurrences of tardiness in a calendar year).

☐   ☐   I demonstrate simple and thoughtful gestures:

- "Hello" in the morning, "Good bye" in the afternoon.

- "Please" and "Thank You."

- "How's your dad? Is he feeling any better?"

☐   ☐   I meet employees at the door when they return from a long vacation or disability and say, "Welcome back. We really missed you."

☐   ☐   I am accessible and approachable. I let employees know when and how to reach me when I am away from the work unit.

☐   ☐   I schedule one-on-one meetings with employees on a regular basis. In these meetings I acknowledge their strengths, discuss developmental needs and ask them for ideas on how to improve the quality of performance and morale on the work unit.

Yes   No

☐   ☐   On occasion, I take informal breaks with employees. I show interest in them as people, not just employees.

Comment:

Ensure that you don't continuously take breaks with the same people or that you aren't perceived to be a member of a clique. Don't get so close to employees on a personal basis that you are expected to understand (condone) when they don't effectively perform their work.

Yes   No

☐   ☐   At each work unit meeting, I have employees single out other members of the team who recently did something above and beyond their job description to exceed a co-worker's expectations.

☐   ☐   On an annual basis, I have employees take turns acknowledging one another for the contributions each has made to the success of the work unit. One by one, I allow each employee to become the focus of attention, receiving compliments from other team members for the strengths they bring to the work unit.

☐   ☐   I periodically facilitate an Appreciative Inquiry (AI) session. I ask employees to focus on the positive aspects of the workplace by brainstorming what they enjoy about the organization, work unit, job and the customers they serve.

Yes   No

☐   ☐   Whenever possible, I tailor my recognition
strategies to each individual employee.

Comment:

What is reinforcing to one person could be aversive to someone else. For example, according to some employees, more responsibility as a reward for outstanding performance may be truly appreciated. It shows that you trust them and believe in their capacity for professional development. Giving other employees additional responsibility as a reward may be viewed as punishment. The employees may remark, "Is this the thanks we get for doing good work? More work? Thanks, but no thanks. We are perfectly content with what we're doing."

An Employee Recognition Planning Worksheet

Name any employees who have recently done something of merit.

_____

_____

_____

_____

_____

Describe what they did and the positive impact it had on others. Include specific behaviors they demonstrated.

_____

_____

_____

_____

Develop a strategy to show your appreciation:

Should the recognition be: ☐ oral ☐ written ☐ both

Should the recognition be: ☐ private ☐ public

Should my manager play a role in recognizing the employee?
☐ Yes ☐ No

If Yes, in what capacity?

_____

_____

Should the Human Resources Department be notified?
☐ Yes ☐ No

If the answer is Yes, for what purpose?

_____

_____

_____

Discussion Questions

Are your employees in a state of psychological deprivation when it comes to recognition? If the answer is yes, what will you do differently to demonstrate appreciation?

_____

_____

_____

_____

_____

_____

What can you do to recognize group accomplishments?

_____

_____

_____

_____

_____

_____

_____

Do your employees provide recognition to each other on an individual or group basis? What can you do to encourage this activity?

_____

_____

_____

_____

_____

_____

In what ways does your work unit have fun?

_____

_____

_____

_____

_____

_____

_____

IV

A FOCUS ON EMPLOYEE SELECTION

Getting ahead in a difficult profession requires avid faith in yourself. That is why some people with mediocre talent, but with great inner drive, go much further than people with vastly superior talent.

Sophia Loren

HIRE FOR ATTITUDE, TRAIN FOR SKILL

The employees you select to be members of your team are a direct reflection on you and your values. In fact, the three most important management decisions you may ever make are:

- Whom you hire.

- Whom you promote.

- Whom you allow to remain on the team.

You may be an enlightened leader with a well-developed strategic plan for your work unit, but unless you have the right players in the most strategic positions, your team will never realize its full potential.

You may be short-staffed and desperate for a warm body. But don't let this be an excuse to lower your selection standards. Sometimes nobody is better than anybody.

Good employees on your work unit would rather work without someone for a sustained period of time than have to put up with an incompetent or toxic personality. All it takes is one exceedingly negative person to control your team culture in a very insidious way.

Look for Emotional Intelligence (EQ)

You can almost always enhance new employees' technical skills by providing training that is tailored to their developmental needs. But you probably don't have the time or ability to change employees' personalities or Emotional Intelligence (EQ). For example, it requires a great deal of concentrated effort to teach:

- Empathy for others.

- Self-control under stressful conditions.

- Social or interpersonal relationship skills.

- Trustworthiness, character or integrity.

- High tolerance for diversity.

- Patience (the ability to defer immediate gratification to achieve a long-term objective).

You may know people who are very smart and who possess advanced degrees but who lack common sense and don't know how to work well with others. These are people with low EQ. And Emotional Intelligence is a better predictor of job success than Intelligence Quotient (IQ).

Therefore, even if candidates for employment are technically competent and experienced, do not hire those who:

- Have a bad attitude.

- Lack a strong work or service ethic.

- Display little enthusiasm or self-motivation.

- Possess a dogmatic/judgmental personality.

On the other hand, you may want to consider hiring candidates who lack specific technical skills and experience providing they:

- Know what they don't know.

- Have the willingness and capacity to learn.

- Possess strong self-management skills (will do the right thing when no one is looking).

- Demonstrate effective social skills.

- Are people of sound character/integrity.

- Are patient (can defer immediate gratification to achieve long-term objectives).

Preparing for the Interview

Identify Qualities for Success

Before you are ready to interview candidates for employment, you must determine the behavioral characteristics necessary to successfully perform the job. There are six practical methods to do this:

1. Examine the job description to determine the Key Results Areas for the position and the necessary skills to be successful.

2. Identify your best performers within this job classification. Develop a list of traits that make them successful.

3. Interview your best performers within the job classification. Ask them to share with you the skill sets and values that make them successful. Have them identify specific challenging situations in which they frequently find themselves and what they do to effectively manage these difficult situations.

4. Interview people from other job classifications who will be working with the selected candidate. Ask them to share with you their perceived needs and expectations of the person who will occupy this position.

5. If you are interviewing to fill a management position, ask employees to share with you the qualities they are looking for in their next supervisor.

6. Ask yourself: "What are those behavioral characteristics that I am most comfortable with in an employee?" For example, do you want a self-starter who is not afraid to take calculated risks? Or do you prefer someone who, when in doubt, asks you for direction before taking action? Would you be comfortable with someone who might eventually want your position? Or would you prefer someone who will be content in this role for the foreseeable future?

You may also want to consider using a selection panel to assist you in identifying what qualities to look for, interview candidates and help you choose the best available person for the job. The panel serves in an advisory capacity. You make the final call on who gets hired.

Three Specific Characteristics to Consider

In addition to identifying the necessary qualities to succeed within a specific job classification, there are generic traits to look for in a candidate. Once you have identified these traits, you are ready to develop interview questions to determine if the candidate possesses these qualities. You should also identify the ideal responses to the questions so that you can compare the answers of the various candidates you interview.

Listed below are three key traits and the behaviors associated with them. Also included are questions you can ask to determine if the candidate possesses these qualities, along with the ideal responses to these questions.

Customer Service Skills

Characteristics to Consider:

- Can identify their customers (both internal and external).

- Can list the specific needs and expectations of each customer.

- Gets a genuine kick out of serving others and is motivated to exceed their expectations.

- Demonstrates active listening skills and empathy for customers' feelings.

- Accurately interprets customers' nonverbal behaviors.

- Remains cool, calm and collected when dealing with upset or demanding customers.

- Effectively educates, negotiates or sets limits with difficult customers.

Question:

"If hired, please identify the customers that you will be serving."

Desired Candidate Response:

Look for an answer that indicates the candidate's awareness of both internal customers (co-workers) and external customers (end users).

Question:

"What are some of the needs and expectations of external customers? What are the criteria they use to evaluate the quality of service?"

Desired Candidate Response:

Look for an answer indicating awareness that customers judge employees as much or more by their human relations skills as by their technical competence. The response should also include those behaviors that demonstrate courtesy, respect and dignity toward all customers.

Question:

"In previous jobs, how have you handled demanding or upset customers?"

Desired Candidate Response:

Look for an answer that indicates a nonjudgmental response to customers' behaviors—an awareness that there is no such thing as a "good" or "bad" customer. Some may be more difficult than others, but it's not the employee's role to judge or label the customer. It's the employee's job to serve the customer the best way possible given the situation that presents itself.

Also look for a response indicating the candidate understands that employees are not entitled to go "toe-to toe" with the customer. If the customer yells at you, you can't yell back. If the customer swears, you can't swear back. The employee is being paid to be cool, calm and collected, particularly under stressful situations.

It's easy to be nice when the customer is nice to you. We all tend to give what we get. But your professionalism and skill set are really put to the test when the customer is acting in an inappropriate manner. Rather than getting frustrated, the employee should see the situation as a professional challenge and an opportunity to set things right.

Finally, look for an awareness that when customers are upset, their primary need is to be heard and understood, not necessarily agreed with. Therefore, getting personally defensive will only make things worse. Customers' perceptions and expectations (right or wrong) are real and legitimate to them. It's the employee's job to deal with customers' feelings in a manner that achieves a win-win outcome.

Question:

"Please describe a good listener."

Desired Candidate Response:

Look for a response that includes some of the following steps:

- Summarize and confirm what you heard the customer say.

- Apologize for inconvenience or frustration (whether or not you are responsible for it).

- Establish boundaries as appropriate.

- When necessary, educate the customer on why you can't do what is requested.

- Provide realistic options to the customer's request. Negotiate strategies and time frames to meet customer's needs.

- Refer the customer to your manager if the situation is getting out of hand.

- Follow up with the customer to ensure that needs have been met.

Question:

"Tell me about a time when you went above and beyond to exceed a customer's expectations."

Desired Candidate Response:

In addition to the verbal response, observe the candidate's facial expression and tone of voice. Does the person convey enthusiasm in describing how he impressed the customer with outstanding service?

After listening to the response, consider asking the candidate a couple more probing questions:

- "Why do you think your approach was effective?"

- "What would have been an ineffective way to handle the situation?"

Question:

"Tell me about a time when you could not meet the customer's expectations. How did you handle the situation?"

Desired Candidate Response:

Look for the candidate's ability to practice successful service recovery—that is, to make the customer feel whole again before a lasting negative impression is made. Also look for creativity, spontaneity, empathy and common sense in response to a difficult customer situation.

Question:

"What would you do if you thought a work unit policy was not conducive to outstanding customer service?"

Desired Candidate Response:

Look for indications that the candidate took the initiative, shared the problem with the manager or raised the issue at a team meeting, and offered practical suggestions for changing the policy.

Question:

"Tell me about a time when you had to say No to a customer's request because it was against policy. How did you handle it?"

Desired Candidate Response:

Look for indications that the candidate patiently explained the reasons behind the policy and offered alternative ways to meet the customer's expectations.

Teamwork Skills

Characteristics to Consider:

- Consistently comes prepared to work as the schedule requires.

- Makes offers of assistance to co-workers in need of help without being asked.

- Politely asks for help.

- Facilitates new employees' success.

- Demonstrates unconditional respect and courtesy toward co-workers.

- Effectively manages conflict with co-workers.

- Appropriately sets limits with aggressive or passive-aggressive co-workers.

Question:

"If hired, is there anything that would prevent you from coming to work as the schedule requires on a consistent basis?"

Desired Candidate Response:

The answer should be no. If the candidate does bring up an issue that could contribute to absenteeism or tardiness, you have the right to ask:

- "Can you tell me a little more about this?"

- "What arrangements have you made so this does not cause an attendance problem?"

Question:

"Approximately how many absences of two days or fewer did you incur within the past year?"

"How many incidents of tardiness did you incur within the past year?"

Desired Candidate Response:

Zero to a couple of occurrences. More people get disciplined or fired for poor attendance than any other reason. Therefore, it is a legitimate and necessary line of inquiry during the interview process.

Question:

"Please describe for me a conflict that you had with a co-worker." After the candidate describes the nature of the conflict, ask a series of follow up questions:

- "How did you respond?"

- "Why did you choose this response?"

- "What was the result?"

- "If you could take anything back, what would you do differently?"

Desired Candidate Response:

Look for a response that indicates the candidate, although provoked, took complete responsibility for effectively managing the situation, talked directly and respectfully to the co-worker and demonstrated willingness to facilitate resolution.

Questions:

"Describe the leadership style of the best manager you ever worked with."

"Describe the characteristics of the worst manager you ever worked with."

Desired Candidate Response:

Look for a response that indicates realistic expectations of the manager. The desirable management characteristics that are identified by the candidate should be a good match with your leadership style.

During the interview, does the person spend a great deal of time criticizing a past manager? This kind of response suggests that the candidate lacks discretion and may have difficulty dealing with authority.

Questions:

"Please provide an example of a time when you disagreed with your manager." After the candidate describes the nature and scope of the conflict, ask him a series of follow up questions:

- "How did you address the problem?"

- "What was the result?"

- "If you could do anything differently what would it be?"

Desired Candidate Response:

Look for an answer that indicates self-reflection and the ability to package ideas in collaborative and constructive manner.

Technical Competence

Qualities to Consider:

- Possesses the requisite knowledge and skill set to perform all aspects of the job.

- Has identified knowledge and skill deficits.

- Has taken full advantage of learning opportunities.

Questions:

"Please tell me why you are qualified for this job. Refer to your knowledge, skills and experience."

"Please share with me the technical requirements contained in the job description in which you feel most confident and skilled."

"In which technical responsibilities contained in the job description do you feel the least confident or skilled?"

"If I were to give you training dollars within the first year of employment for you to develop your technical skills, how would you spend them?"

Desired Candidate Response:

Look for a response that makes you believe that the candidate has the knowledge, skills and experience to carry out the responsibilities as described in the job description. If the candidate does not currently have the ideal skill sets to perform the job, make the following assessment:

- Can you build on the person's strengths while shoring up weaknesses?

- Does the person have the *willingness* to learn the technical skills?

- Does the person have the *capacity* to learn the technical skills?

- Do you have the time and resources to develop the person?

- What is the quality of your work unit's new employee orientation process?

Exercise to Evaluate Candidate's Responses

Consider asking the following additional questions to assess the candidate's EQ. After you read each question, identify an ideal candidate response.

Questions:

"If asked, what would your last manager say about you?" Or...

"What did your manager say are your strengths and opportunities for improvement on your most recent performance appraisal?"

Desired Candidate Response:

_____

_____

_____

Question:

"Please describe how you like to be managed."

Desired Candidate Response:

_____

_____

_____

Question:

"Describe the perfect work environment."

Desired Candidate Response:

_____

_____

_____

Question:

"Describe the characteristics of an ideal co-worker."

Desired Candidate Response:

_____

_____

_____

Question:

"Describe the characteristics of the worst employee you ever had to work with."

Desired Candidate Response:

_____

_____

_____

Question:

"How would past co-workers describe you?"

Desired Candidate Response:

_____

_____

_____

Question:

"Why are you interested in this position?"

Desired Candidate Response:

_____

_____

_____

Question:

"Why do you think you are qualified for this position?"

Desired Candidate Response:

_____

_____

_____

Other Important Qualities to Look For in a Candidate

In addition to how candidates respond to specific interview questions, pay close attention to their nonverbal communication. Carefully observe:

- How the candidates relate to others in the office before and after the job interview

- How the candidates introduce themselves and conclude the interview

- Firmness of handshake

- Courtesy and friendliness

- Poise

- Confidence

- Enthusiasm

- Tone of voice

- Volume control

- Facial expressions

- Eye contact

- Attire

Also look for how prepared the candidates are for the interview:

- How much do they know about the organization, industry, work unit and job?

- Have they prepared appropriate questions for you?

- Do they appear hesitant for you to speak with their former employers?

It is critical that you carefully examine all candidates' job applications:

- Are they complete?

- Are they neat?

- Are there glaring employment gaps that can't be adequately explained?

- Do candidates appear to change jobs on a frequent basis? If yes, can they explain the apparent lack of stability?

If You Hire, Can You Fire?

Some candidates have mastered the fine art of interviewing. They are poised, articulate, organized and thorough in response to your questions. They appear to be the answer to your prayers. But after you hire them and observe them in action, you realize that you have been mislead. You thought that you were employing Dr. Jekyll, but you got Mr. Hyde.

Most employees are on their best behavior during the first 90 days of employment. So if you don't like their quality of performance during this period of time, it's only likely to get worse. Assess the reasons why they are failing to meet your expectations:

- Is it because they lack specific skills? Provide training and development.

- Is it because they lack confidence? Offer encouragement and support.

- Is it a system or resource problem? Remove obstacles to success.

- Is there role ambiguity? Clarify who is responsible for what. Ensure that they understand how their job begins, ends and overlaps with other members of the team.

- Do they lack the capacity to succeed and/or the intrinsic motivation (will) to succeed? Own up to your hiring mistake and cut your losses early. It is generally easier to terminate a short-term employee than someone who has been employed within the organization for a sustained period of time. And the unemployment compensation liability will not be as significant.

Pre-Interview Worksheet

Before you interview candidates, identify the specific traits you're looking for, questions to determine if the candidate has those traits, and desired answers to the interview questions. Use this worksheet to organize your thoughts.

Experience, Knowledge, Skills, Attitudes and Values Necessary to Meet Job Requirements	Interview Questions to Determine if Candidate Possesses These Qualities	Desired Candidate Response

Discussion Questions

Do you agree with the statement, "Whom you hire, promote and keep on your team are the three most important decisions you will ever make?" Please explain.

_____

_____

_____

Do you engage in a structured planning process as described above before you actually interview job candidates? Please describe.

_____

_____

_____

_____

Do you ask the same questions of all job candidates? Are your questions directly related to the responsibilities contained in the job description? Do you know what responses you're looking for before you ask the questions? Please explain.

_____

_____

_____

_____

BOOK SUMMARY

The Best Practices of Engaged leaders:

Articulate a set of values, clarify objectives and pull people together in pursuit of a common vision.

Convert work unit values into standards of conduct. For example, what does outstanding customer service or teamwork look like in behavioral terms?

Develop a user-friendly monitoring and evaluation system to "inspect what you expect."

Align your everyday activities with your values. Spend quality time on your work unit engaged with employees and customers. If necessary, informally negotiate with your manager on how to make the best use of your time.

Establish your credibility as a leader. Win support and influence people by demonstrating intelligence, character and good will. Demonstrate that you are worthy of belief and confidence. Model the attitude and behaviors expected of employees.

Maintain a retribution-free communication environment. Encourage employees to play the role of devil's advocate without fear of retaliation.

Listen to employees. Include them in decision making processes whenever possible.

Share information with employees so they understand the context in which they are performing their jobs.

Be a spokesperson and advocate for your employees. Support them under fire. Watch their backs.

Coach, counsel, train and develop your employees. Create a learning culture.

Delegate as appropriate. You can't do everything yourself.

Care for your employees. Don't take care of them.

Place resources in employees' hands, remove system barriers that serve as an obstacle to their success and hold them accountable for outstanding results.

Help employees separate problems from realities. Focus on obstacles to success that are within your immediate and direct control to overcome.

Don't tolerate employees' complaints about things that no one can do anything about. Understand that complaining only leads to more negativity and a sense of victimization and entitlement.

Don't waste time on meetings that are inefficient, dysfunctional or counterproductive. Clarify participants' roles and decision making authority before you begin deliberations.

Teach employees effective problem solving and conflict management skills and hold them accountable for direct and respectful communications. Conduct role clarification and role negotiation sessions to ensure cooperation within and between job classifications, shifts and work units.

Ensure that work unit policies and procedures are user-friendly for both employees and customers.

Recognize employees for achievement on both an individual and team basis.

Understand that the three most important management decisions you will ever make are whom you hire, whom you promote and whom you allow to remain on the team. Appreciate that no matter how desperate you are for a warm body, sometimes nobody is better than anybody. Therefore, hold out until you find the right person for the job.

Hire for attitude and train for skill. When considering a candidate for employment, look for a strong work ethic, service orientation, self-motivation and positive attitude.

Remember that nobody is entitled to a job. Team membership is not a right. It's a privilege, and with this privilege comes specific responsibilities and conditions of employment:

- Strong technical/clinical competence

- Outstanding customer service

- A commitment to teamwork

- Fiscal prudence

REFERENCES

Aristotle. (2006). *On rhetoric: A theory of civil discourse.(2nd ed.).* A translation by George A. Kennedy. New York: Oxford University Press, USA.

Cohen, M. H. (2008). *The power of self-management.* Minneapolis, MN: Creative Health Care Management.

Cohen, M. H. (2006). *What you accept is what you teach.* Minneapolis, MN: Creative Health Care Management.

Covey, S. R. (1994). *First things first.* New York: Simon and Schuster.

Creative Health Care Management. (2007). *Leading an empowered organization participant manual.* Minneapolis, MN: Author.

Goleman, D. (2000). *Working with emotional intelligence.* New York: Bantam Books.

Harrison, R. (1972). When power conflicts trigger team spirit. *European Business*, Spring.

Heider, J. (1985). *The tao of leadership: Lau Tzu's tao te ching adapted for a new age.* New York: Bantam Books.

Tannenbaum, R. & Schmidt, W. (1958). How to choose a leadership pattern. *Harvard Business Review*, March-April.

ABOUT MICHAEL HENRY COHEN

Mike Cohen is a nationally recognized workshop leader and consultant specializing in leadership and team development, organizational communications, employee relations, conflict management and customer service. He has taught Interpersonal Communications, Group Process and Organizational Behavior at Northwestern, Roosevelt and Dominican Universities, and conducts leadership effectiveness programs for organizations throughout the United States.

Mike served as Director of Employee Relations and Development and Vice President of Human Resources at Weiss Memorial Hospital, Chicago, for 12 years. He holds a Master of Arts degree in Communication Studies from Northwestern University. His the author of numerous articles and three previous books, *On-the-Job Survival Guide*, *What You Accept is What You Teach* and *The Power of Self Management*.

Information on Michael H. Cohen's management and employee development workshops can be obtained by perusing his web page, www.michaelhcohenconsulting.com, or by writing to:

Michael H. Cohen
333 N. Euclid Avenue • Oak Park, IL 60302
708.386.1968 • canoepress@yahoo.com

Books by MICHAEL H. COHEN

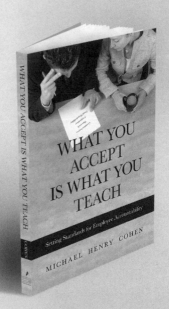

This book provides practical advice to managers on how to hold employees accountable for a strong work ethic, intrinsic motivation, a positive attitude and constructive conduct toward customers and co-workers. It describes a leader's rights and responsibilities relative to maintaining standards for teamwork and customer service. It discusses how to effectively confront and set limits with employees who demonstrate counter productive and passive-aggressive behaviors that raise havoc on group morale. Over 20,000 copies sold. Softcover, 183 pages. (2007)

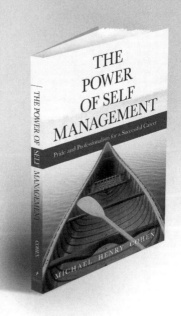

This practical employee companion to **What You Accept is What You Teach** helps staff prepare themselves for the constantly changing health care environment. Learn how to be an outstanding "Organizational Citizen" by developing effective problem solving and "Change-Agent" skills. Develop conflict resolution competence and assertive "Fair-Fighting" skills to deal with difficult co-workers, managers and physicians. Empower yourself to take complete responsibility for your own job success, satisfaction, intrinsic motivation, work and service ethic—regardless of the environment you work in. Great for all staff! Softcover, 159 pages. (2008)

ORDER FORM

1. Call toll-free 800.728.7766 x111 and use your Visa, Mastercard or American Express or a company purchase order

2. Fax your order to: 952.854.1866

3. Mail your order with pre-payment or company purchase order to:

   Creative Health Care Management
   5610 Rowland Road, Suite 100
   Minneapolis, MN 55343
   Attn: Resources Department

CREATIVE
HEALTH CARE
MANAGEMENT

4. Order Online at: www.chcm.com, click on Resources.

Product	Price	Quantity	Subtotal	TOTAL
B605: *Time to Lead*	$19.95			
B519: *The Power of Self Management*	$15.00			
B558: *What You Accept is What You Teach*	$16.00			
B563: *Employee Handbook for On the Job Survival*	$6.95			
Shipping Costs: 1 book = $6.00, 2-9 = $8.00, 10 or more = $10.00 *Call for express rates*				
Order TOTAL				

Need more than one copy? We have quantity discounts available.

Quantity Discounts (Books Only)		
10–49 = 10% off	50–99 = 20% off	100 or more = 30% off

Payment Methods: ☐ Credit Card   ☐ Check   ☐ Purchase Order PO# _____

Credit Card	Number			Expiration	AVS (3 digits)
Visa / Mastercard / American Express	–	–	–	/	
Cardholder address (if different from below):	Signature:				

Customer Information	
Name:	
Title:	
Company:	
Address:	
City, State, Zip:	
Daytime Phone:	
Email:	

Satisfaction guarantee: If you are not satisfied with your purchase, simply return the products within 30 days for a full refund.
For a free catalog of all our products, visit www.chcm.com or call 800.728.7766 x111.